# ACCOUNTABILITY
# LEADERSHIP

*What did you think*

*How apply*

# INTRODUCTION
# The Importance of Accountability

*"Break the riddle of accountability, the thinking goes, and you
will have solved one of the thorniest issues in modern business."*

Mihnea Moldoveanu from
*"The Promise: The Basic Building Block of Accountability,"*
(Rotman Magazine, Fall 2009).

Ask anyone in charge of managing people to define their
number one leadership challenge, and they're likely to tell
you that it's achieving accountability for performance. CEOs, top
executive teams, managers, and line supervisors all struggle to
get the right things done, the right way, by the right staff, at the
right time. When goals are met or exceeded, everyone's a hero. But
even the very best organisations face unforeseen challenges and
sometimes fail to meet their goals. At such times the organisation
must quickly be put on the right track, and this cannot be done
without a strong culture of accountability.

Whether I'm working as a senior executive, a consultant, or executive coach in organisations, I consistently witness how fractures within individual, team, and cultural accountability inevitably lead to unrealised opportunities and poor business effectiveness. Across the gamut of businesses—manufacturing, service, non-profit, government, global and small businesses—leaders find it challenging to motivate and inspire people to give their best work.

Cultures low in accountability demonstrate behaviours that undermine business results through silence, fear, blame, collusion, resistance, and deflection of responsibility. Companies enable dysfunctional cultures through structures such as organisational silos, cumbersome bureaucratic hierarchies, and entitlement-based policies.

Unchecked, such behaviours and systems contribute to the following problems:

- **Poor performance**—In the 1980s, American CIA agent Aldrich Ames sold US government secrets to the Soviet KGB, allowing a significant breach of national security. His actions can be traced in part to the CIA's fundamental inability to hold employees to account for their performance.

- **Lack of trust**—Following an enquiry into Ames's activities, it was perceived that CIA Director James Woolsey failed in his responsibility to implement appropriate consequences that would rectify the organisation's systemic problems with accountability. Trust in the directors' capacity to hold the organisation to account was significantly undermined, and he was forced to resign.

- **Missed deadlines and cost overruns**—Consistent with many flawed private public partnerships around the world, executives at the William Osler Health Centre in Ontario were over-confident and over-optimistic at the outset of negotiating a big hospital project with the Health Infrastructure Company of Canada. Executives failed to challenge initial assumptions, and failed to hold the service provider to account with respect to cost overruns as high as $550 million, together with an additional $147 million in capital costs and significant reductions in the planned hospital's dimensions. The program was delivered late while the detailed financial arrangements remained undisclosed and unaccountable to the public under the guise of "commercial in confidence."

- **Questionable ethics**—From 2002-2005, surveys by the Centre for Academic Integrity of 50,000 students across eighty-three college campuses in the US and Canada revealed that 70% of undergraduate students admitted to cheating and 41% of faculty members who were aware of student cheating did nothing, setting the stage in a student's formative years for future unethical and unaccountable behaviour in business.

- **Chronic inefficiency**—In its work with developing countries, The Medicines Transparency Alliance found that lack of transparency and accountability on the price, availability, quality, and promotion of medicines led to price hikes, inadequate forecasting and short supply, increased spoilage and theft due to inefficient storage, and wastage of products that were over-ordered and were beyond their use-by date.

- **Poor customer satisfaction**—After a series of documented incidents involving stuck accelerators, Toyota was slow to accept responsibility and to recall millions of cars. The company's tepid response and poor transparency damaged its reputation and stock value, and led to its losing its number one position in the global auto market.

- **Poor safety**—Several rooms at Norwich and Norfolk University Hospital that were used to contain patients with lethal viruses such as tuberculosis were found to be defective. Following an investigation by the National Audit Office it was determined that both hospital management and Octagon Healthcare (the consortium that constructed and operated the hospital) knew of the defects for at least two years, but each had taken the position that the other party should be held accountable for the problem.

When leaders fail to hold people accountable for performance, and when they seemingly allow or reward wrong behaviours, everyone suffers. Low morale is contagious and spreads like a virus throughout the organisation.

It affects team performance, essentially infecting and destroying motivation. With low accountability, adversarial positions are easily triggered, leading in some cases to industrial dispute.

Worse still, cultures low in accountability have contributed to some of the most devastating crises and business failures—for example, the 1986 space shuttle Challenger explosion, the 2001 Enron bankruptcy, the global financial crisis of 2008, the Fukushima nuclear disaster in 2011, and the 2012 sinking of the Costa Concordia cruise ship.

In every instance, the public inquiries that followed these disasters demonstrated a strong causal link to failures in accountability.

## The Case for Accountability Leadership

Here's what's clear to me: Business leaders who employ the principles of leadership accountability stand to multiply their chances of success and market leadership. Managers and their companies who have implemented such an approach report high performing characteristics such as:

- Cross-functional teams are the norm and are aligned, flexible, and adaptive to change.

- Individuals and teams have a sense of ownership, and are focused, disciplined and collaborative, while holding each other accountable for outcomes.

- Employee-manager communications are engaging, high trust, and free flowing.

- Instead of entitlement, fear, and change resistance, organisational policies are driven by accountability, trust, and continuous improvement.

- Striving for excellence in customer service is embedded as a core business value.

- Company-wide culture embraces learning. It's fun, friendly, and meaningful, and delivers great results.

The case for improved accountability in leadership has become critical for any leader with pragmatic desires for better business success.

## The Rhetoric Doesn't Match the Reality

For many leaders, motivating human beings toward organisational goals is mysteriously complex. Leaders know their jobs well, their areas of expertise, but they're not psychologists or behavioural scientists. Some leaders are just plain uncomfortable dealing in the realm of human nature.

I've known many leaders who are truly exceptional human beings. They're highly intelligent—both intellectually and emotionally— they're experts in their fields, and they have charismatic personalities that charm most individuals and groups.

Indeed, they carry a lot of influence and power. Almost all I speak with, however, express a desire to do a better job leading their people. Despite their best efforts, some leaders aren't touching the hearts and minds of people in order to inspire greater engagement. Still others are engaging and inspirational without getting execution and the results they need. There's a knowing-doing gap no matter what they try.

The truth is that most leaders can learn to improve accountability, both in themselves and with their teams, and they can create a culture of accountability throughout their organisations.

It would be hard to find a leader who does not claim to support the case for improved accountability, yet most leaders fall short, leaving unrealised potential for business success. Leaders at all levels continue to use incentives that don't work well, and fail to use ones that are known to work extremely well. Here are some reasons why:

- Leaders assume they already know how to motivate and engage people, so they don't explore their own shortcomings in this area.

- Leaders persist in using traditional command and control methods, which have proven ineffective with knowledge workers.

- Leaders continue to tolerate behaviour unaligned with goals and by default reward misaligned behaviour.

Each of these behavioural patterns stems from the unconscious mind: Leaders aren't aware when they're doing them, and therefore they can't work on changing these habits. Unless such leaders are proactively working to update their accountability skills with an executive coach, they aren't likely to bring these self-defeating habits into conscious awareness.

## What You'll Find Here

In this book I present the reasons for lack of accountability, outline three guiding principles, and make suggestions that will help leaders improve their use of accountability for successful outcomes.

It's my goal that by developing and presenting practical, down-to-earth ideas in this book on Leadership Accountability, we can make the leader's job of getting results that much easier, or at least comprehensively streamlined through an Accountability Plan.

An Accountability Plan essentially outlines a system of accountability designed to pull the disparate pieces of human motivation together. We need to form a better picture of accountability that actually works so that everyone can achieve stellar results.

It's not enough to bring in motivational speakers that leave people feeling enthusiastic and energised for an hour or a few days. Even the most inspirational mission statements and company incentives have their limits.

## The Foundation for Accountability Leadership

In my experience, based on working with hundreds of leaders and thousands of people in organisations, as well as reviewing the leading authors on accountability, what's needed in an Accountability Plan boils down to three foundational principles:

- Clarity of purpose, mission and strategy along with clear goals.

- Compelling consequences, both for encouragement and discouragement.

- Culture of accountability, evident in attitudes and conversations and sustained through systems.

These three principles are discussed for how each contributes to accountability leadership. We will also review motivational theory and best practices for bringing out the best in the people you lead.

## How's Your Accountability Leadership?

Take a look at how these principles are applied on three levels:

1. **For leaders:** How are their own behaviours contributing to accountability? What clear messages do they need to convey?

2. **For individuals and teams:** What works for motivating and influencing high performance? What are the compelling consequences that truly work?

3. **For the organisation:** What conversations, mindset and systems are required for the culture to support and sustain accountability?

### YOUR ACCOUNTABILITY PLAN

In the pipeline is the *Accountability Leadership Field Guide* to provide checklists and questions in order to think through the major accountability concepts I discuss here.

The Field Guide will help you apply the lessons I describe in this book by developing a strategy for change accompanied by an Accountability Plan of action. Your Plan will set out a series of steps tailored to the performance and accountability challenges of your organisation. These steps I refer to as your *"accountability code®"*.

Reflect on each of these levels—leaders, teams and organisational culture—and consider where you would rate your organisation on a scale of one to three where one is poor, 2 is average and 3 is great. It may be helpful to look at your own organisation's accountability by estimating on a scale of one to three (poor = 1, average = 2, great = 3) the level of participation in each principle at each level, as in the following matrix:

| | Leaders | Individuals | Organisation |
|---|---|---|---|
| Clear messages | | | |
| Compelling Consequences | | | |
| Culture: Conversations/ mindset/ systems | | | |

Some question whether people can realistically change their behaviours, especially when it comes to ingrained work habits and attitudes. I say, yes, they absolutely can!

No matter what level of responsibilities you have in a company, you'll find greater job satisfaction and meaning when you explore and apply the ideas of accountability.

**In the Appendix:** Here you'll find a list of helpful books and resources including interviews with authors and expert leaders on creating accountability that works.

I am grateful for all the work and research published by leading experts. I've tried to summarise their work keeping their terminologies intact yet explaining their theories as simply and clearly as possible.

I've interviewed key experts on the subject of accountability and you'll find information to access the audio files.

## Good Ideas Aren't Good Enough

My wish is that by reading this book, you'll identify areas where you can improve your leadership accountability. More than that, I hope you'll not rest satisfied by the discovery of "good ideas."

Why? I say this because "good ideas" don't last. When they turn into hard work, they get abandoned by the very people who need them the most.

Don't let this happen to you. Take action; put these good ideas into your daily leadership strategies and into a tangible, measurable Accountability Plan for personal and organisational improvement. After all, what gets measured gets done!

Like many leadership development specialists who work with smart executives, I encourage you to be among the small percentage who muster the courage to take on this challenging work of accountability improvement.

You'll be glad you did, because you'll see the results clearly. It's not some vague feel-good approach to an empathy-based management fad of the month.

This is real. This works. It always has, only the key required elements have slightly changed with the evolving nature of 21st century business, economics, and knowledge workers.

If you think things are tough now, you may not be prepared for the accelerating pace ahead. Read this now, and then do what you need to do. Call your coach. Make a plan, start improving your leadership accountability and the accountability culture of your organisation.

Here's to your successful Leadership Accountability journey. Let's get started!

*Di Worrall*

# CHAPTER 1

## Accountability for Leaders

As a leader, how can you influence more of your people to step up to the plate, see opportunities, and take ownership, rather than get by with minimal effort?

When you observe your superstars, you see how effectively they engage in their work. How can you get more of your people to be like them?

Increasing staff engagement may seem simple in concept, but it's not so simple in its practical application. This chapter reveals what you can do as a leader to help your staff work better and feel more engaged and satisfied with work. You do this by creating conditions of accountability. In the long run, they'll thank you for it.

I believe that the vast majority of working people crave opportunities to find renewed enthusiasm and energy in their jobs. Most employees—those who are neither stars nor problem hires—respond well to challenges and stretch goals with the right leadership.

## ACCOUNTABILITY VS. RESPONSIBILITY

The literature defines accountability and responsibility in various ways. In this book, I use the definition of accountability that refers to the capacity of one person to hold another to account for the delivery of their promises.

Responsibility, on the other hand is one's individual capacity to deliver on the promises they make.

Organisations require competency in both in order to achieve a healthy and productive "high accountability" culture.

Which begs the question: How do you reach the hearts and minds of the people working for you and ignite their enthusiasm and energy so they bring their best to work each day?

## Accountability Starts at the Top

As a leader, accountability starts with you. You have a weighted relationship with your people. What you say, what you do, and even those things you don't say or do, have a far greater impact on the people in your sphere of influence than you might think.

Your employees look to you not only for the big decisions, but also for the finer nuances of acceptable cultural norms in how to feel, how to behave, and how to respond. It's crucial that you take your own responsibility and accountability seriously.

This means you take responsibility without becoming overly responsible. Yes, you are responsible, especially for failures and mistakes. And yet you are expected to give the credit to others, to the teams and the individuals who do the work.

You are responsible for getting results through others. You can't do that without creating conditions of accountability in the organisation you lead.

How you handle accountability will determine how willingly your staff will accept your leadership. How much trust they will grant you will be earned by how well you handle these two key issues:

1. Accountability for errors, both of your own and of your staff.
2. Credit for successes, both of your own and of your staff.

## A New Perception of Accountability

In organisations, accountability is often viewed as something negative that happens to you when things go wrong. This kind of accountability never works over the long term. Real accountability is achieved through a step-by-step process that makes things go right.

Accountability should not be defined as punishment for mistakes. Rather, it's a powerful, positive, and enabling principle that provides a foundation to build both individual and company success.

The way we hold one another accountable defines the nature of our working relationships, how we interact, and what we expect from one another. With positive accountability, people embrace their individual roles in facilitating change, and they take ownership for making progress happen.

As people adopt a mindset of accountability, they learn that their participation can and will make a big difference. They go the extra mile because they know what to do, and they know how their performance drives results. This adds energy to their work, because, as we've noted, almost all people crave meaning and fulfillment in what they do. (We'll review the studies that show this in Chapter 2.)

Accountability (or the lack thereof) is arguably the single biggest issue confronting organisations today, especially for those engaged in big change initiatives. It is only when you build a culture of accountability that you have people who can and will achieve game-changing results.

Your people need you as their leader to hold them accountable, to show them how to hold each other accountable, and to tell them why their work matters. As leader, you need to clearly communicate how their performance and productivity contribute to superior results.

## Optimise Your Culture

Few managers excel at optimising organisational culture. While they're aware of surveys that reveal two-thirds of employees are disengaged, they don't know how to look at culture and readily identify components. They get lost in emotions, feelings, beliefs, soft skills, and fuzzy thinking.

Optimising your culture for high accountability should command as much attention as performance metrics, operations, finances, sales, and every other typical discipline for monitoring and measuring organisational performance.

By harnessing the power of accountability, you can change the game by growing faster than your competitors, surviving a bad economy, improving your value proposition, and outperforming all previous metrics.

Here is a story from one maverick CEO who turned around his company by putting *Employees First, Customers Second.*

### THE MAJORITY OF WORKERS ARE DISENGAGED

Gallup research makes clear that employee engagement has a strong correlation with key organisational outcomes in any economic climate.

And even during difficult economic times, employee engagement is an important competitive differentiator for organisations.

A current report is based on an unprecedented study of engagement among more than 47,000 employees in 120 countries around the world.

*The overall results indicate that 11% of workers worldwide are engaged.*

In other words, about one in nine employees worldwide are emotionally connected to their workplaces and feel they have the resources and support they need to succeed.

The majority of workers, 62%, are not engaged—that is, emotionally detached and likely to be doing little more than is necessary to keep their jobs.

And 27% are actively disengaged, indicating they view their workplaces negatively and are liable to spread that negativity to others.

## TOP DOWN ACCOUNTABILITY— HCL TECHNOLOGIES PAVES THE WAY

In a revealing article in the June 2010 issue of Harvard Business Review, CEO Vineet Nayar shares how he turned around HCL Technologies in four years. The article, *How I Did It: A Maverick CEO Explains How He Persuaded His Team to Leap into the Future*, offers examples of top-down accountability that starts with the CEO and senior leaders.

When Vineet Nayar was appointed president of the Delhi-based IT services provider HCL Technologies in 2005, the company's revenues were growing by about 30% a year, but it was losing market share and mindshare. Competitors were growing at the rate of 40% or 50% a year, and the IT services industry was changing rapidly.

Customers didn't want to work with an undifferentiated service provider that offered discrete services; they wanted long-term partners that would provide end-to-end services. Nayar asked himself and his team if and how HCL could become such a company.

History will tell you it did. By 2009 HCL had changed its business model, nearly tripled its annual revenues, doubled its market capitalisation, been ranked India's best employer by Hewitt—and pioneered a unique management culture that the CEO calls *Employees First, Customers Second* (EFCS). The details are included in his book with that title.

HCL grew by about 20% in the worst year of the recession. In 2008 they closed orders worth twice as much as those of the previous year and hired hundreds of employees globally, including in the U.S. and the UK.

## What Leaders Can Do

Vineet Nayar, Vice Chairman and CEO of HCL Technologies Ltd., turned things around for his company by emphasising accountability. His first bold move was to make his own 360° performance review available for all to see on the company intranet. He then made the 360° reviews of all managers open to anyone in the organisation.

Nayar took transparency even further, sharing financials with everyone employed. There was also an online portal where managers posted videos of their plans and projects. Open feedback was encouraged. Anyone could open a ticket to make a complaint or a suggestion. Managers were required to respond. Strategic planning became collaborative effort throughout the organisation. Here's what Mr. Nayar says about the process:

"Rather than engage in layoffs or restructuring, I asked employees for ideas to help us get through the bad times. They offered many suggestions. Some of them related to cost cutting, but most of them focused on how to increase revenues. Most important, HCL's employees felt that we had included them in determining how to weather the storm—unlike other IT companies, where, because management didn't take an inclusive approach, employees felt uncertain about their future and that of the organisation."

Our experience has shown that after some initial push back from corporate leaders regarding legitimate concerns such as vexatious reviews, this transparent approach to performance review has proven highly beneficial in that it is generally recognised that the views of the many are a more realistic indication of your true circle of influence (not control) and are more balanced than the views of a select few.

## THE 4 KEYS TO HCL'S TURNAROUND

**1: Mirror Mirror.**

Talk honestly. Face the truth. Enable people to see that a change has to be made.

**2: Create trust through transparency.**

Find ways to build a culture of trust so that people will entertain the plan for change. Share financial data, good and bad, within and across groups. Use transparency as the basis for a new approach to performance reviews and strategic planning.

**3: Invert the organisational pyramid.**

Make support functions and executives accountable to frontline workers, rather than the other way around. Not only does this increase value, but it brings clarity and meaning to the structure.

**4: Recast the CEO's role.**

Transfer the ownership of change from the office of the CEO to employees. Allow the CEO to ask as many questions as he answers.

## Three Guiding Principles to Accountability Leadership

Long before leaders can set up accountability plans for getting others to take on more responsibility and ownership in their work, they must demonstrate their own accountability in their actions. You, as leader, create the conditions necessary for accountability systems to function.

There are three guiding principles every leader needs to address if he or she wants to set the foundation for accountability to be effective throughout the organisation:

1. **Clear and concise communications.** What business are we in? What's our strategy? Mission? Values? How do we translate these into real world goals? What are the tradeoffs that are allowed? The boundaries never to be crossed?

   A clear message helps people know what's expected and how to make the right decisions. Notwithstanding that this is common sense, many employees continue to report that messages are unclear. The opportunity for leaders and managers is to find a better way to communicate expectations clearly.

2. **Compelling consequences.** Accountability is traditionally viewed as a negative consequence that mandates "punishment" for poor performance (a "carrot and stick" mentality). A new definition views accountability as a means to produce positive consequences using accountability systems to work together for better results. Celebrating small wins and progress along the way is becoming a tool of choice for progressive leaders.

Despite the fact that traditional management techniques of command and control and micromanagement have proven ineffective over the last four decades of the modern organisation, these techniques continue to proliferate. Equally ineffective is some leaders' persistent tolerance of poor performance. At both ends of the spectrum lie opportunities for leaders to do a better job creating accountability systems that work including improving the way people are motivated and rewarded for good work.

3. **Culture of accountability.** It starts with a conversation. Leaders set the tone for cultural norms. Conversations are a typical indicator of an organisation's cultural reality. Too many leaders and managers inadvertently fall into common conversational traps that undermine their business goals. Mastering conversations that encourage accountability is how leaders exert a powerful influence on positive cultural change. Such conversations focus on behaviours and reality, and don't shy away from the difficult issues.

Accountability conversations are empowering and focus on: What can be changed? What can't? What's the best choice given reality? How can feedback on failures and mistakes be expressed in a way that's productive?

Here lies an opportunity for leaders to do a better job communicating with their people in a way that fosters trust and engagement and encourages growth and learning.

## START WITH "WHY"

Martin Luther King Jr. and Walt Disney are renowned for communicating their "why"—the reasons they acted, why they cared and their future hopes. Great business leaders follow suit:

- Herb Kelleher, founder of Southwest Airlines, believes air travel should be fun and accessible to everyone.
- Apple's Steve Wozniak and Steve Jobs set out to challenge the established corporations' status quo, believing that everyone should have a computer.
- Walmart's Sam Walton believed people should have access to lowcost goods.
- Starbucks' Howard Schultz wanted to create social experiences in cafés, not just sell a cup of coffee.

## Leadership Communications

How you handle mistakes, blame, feedback, and credit goes a long way to setting the stage for accountability. As a leader, everything you say and do takes on greater meaning, sometimes beyond your intent. Your responsibility lies in using the power of your words to influence behaviours that bring about the right business results.

By the time you've been in a leadership position for even a short period, you quickly become aware of how miscommunication happens. Leadership communication includes everything you say and the way you say it, but also what you omit to say.

You probably wouldn't be in a leadership position without already possessing a high level of skilled communication and political savvy. Here's how you can harness those skills for even greater accountability throughout your organisation.

## Clarity

Nothing is more important than consistently delivering your core message to employees. They depend on you as leader to reiterate what matters most. This includes why you're in business in the first place.

Simon Sinek writes and speaks about this in his TED Talk, "Start with Why." Leaders who want to succeed should clearly communicate what they believe and why they're so passionate about their cause, according Sinek, author of *Start with Why: How Great Leaders Inspire Everyone to Take Action* (Portfolio, 2010).

The more leaders try to inspire their followers through communicating with heart as well as by establishing clear, actionable goals, the more people will want to step up to accountability because they align with core values that truly matter.

## WHY MILLIONS QUIT THEIR JOBS EVERY MONTH

Why do so many people quit their jobs, even in a recession and uncertainty?

- A report from Grow America compiled research from several sources. In truth, the majority of people, quitting or not, are currently unhappy in their corporate jobs.

- A study by Harris Interactive indicates a full 74 percent of people would today consider finding a new job.

- The most recent Mercer's What's Working study says 32 percent are actively looking.

**The reasons for their unhappiness:**

- A recent study by Accenture reports:
    1. They don't like their boss (31%),
    2. A lack of empowerment (31%),
    3. Internal politics (35%) and
    4. Lack of recognition (43%).

## The Power of Praise and Recognition

*A prince should be slow to punish and quick to reward.*

Ovid

Few things have as much power to influence behaviour as when you give praise. Recognition is one of the crucial pieces in the motivation puzzle. As a leader, you have a responsibility to your followers to recognise and reward exceptional performance.

Positive reinforcement is a powerful source of fuel that energises people to try harder, persist longer, and overcome difficulties. We are hard-wired for recognition. When we receive praise, our brain releases dopamine, a neurotransmitter that stimulates the pleasure centers. It's addictive.

The problem is that right now, the majority of us don't give or receive anywhere near the amount of praise that we should.

Many people report they don't receive adequate praise or recognition for their efforts at work. They don't feel appreciated.

And yet a Gallup survey shows that individuals who receive regular recognition and praise:

- Increase their individual productivity.
- Increase engagement among their colleagues.
- Are more likely to stay with their organisation.
- Receive higher loyalty and satisfaction scores from customers.
- Have better safety records and fewer accidents on the job.

In a study conducted by Dr. Gerald Graham of Wichita State University, of sixty-five potential incentives in the workplace the most motivating incentive was simply a manager who "personally congratulates an employee for doing a good job." However, fifty-eight percent of respondents said their manager rarely—if ever—offered simple praise.

Even with this common knowledge, vast numbers of employees still feel underappreciated for their work. Nothing has greater impact on an employee than when recognition comes from their direct supervisor.

For some leaders with busy schedules this may seem impossible. If you're not walking around and in conversation with staff, then you're missing a great opportunity to energise your people. Find out who deserves recognition and then deliver it yourself. You'll be amazed at the effect.

Of course, for feedback of any kind to be well received and have a desired impact, leaders must establish connection to people and gain solid trust.

## Building Trust

You build trust when you communicate your genuine interest in people and their needs, and maintain focus on achieving desired results for the organisation.

While many factors contribute to our perceptions of trustworthiness, three vital traits comprise "the trinity of trust," writes management consultant James Robbins in *Nine Minutes on Monday*:

1. **Character:** What do your employees see when they look at you? How do they perceive your values, work ethic, integrity and honesty? Studies consistently cite honesty as the number one attribute of effective managers—consistently doing what they say they'll do. When managers act with integrity and reliability, they lay a foundation on which employees can rely.

2. **Competence:** Employees place more trust in you when they believe you're capable of effective leadership. This does not mean you're the smartest one in the room—a position of superiority that, in fact, undermines perceived competency. Your managerial competency should not be measured by your technical skills, but by your ability to understand and influence people.

3. **Caring:** The most neglected ingredient in the trust trinity is the ability to show you care. Employees don't want to be cogs in a wheel. They want to feel that they matter and their bosses actually care about them as people. Only then can they reciprocate with trust.

## The Power of Feedback

Authors Barbara Fredrickson and Marcial Losada argue that feedback works best when there are overall more positive than negative comments.

### NEGATIVITY BIAS

Negativity bias is the psychological phenomenon by which humans pay more attention to negative rather than positive experiences or information.

In the brain, the area used for the negativity bias is the amygdala. This specific area uses about two-thirds of its neurons searching for negative experiences.

Positive experiences have to be held in awareness for more than 12 seconds in order for the transfer from short-term memory to longterm memory to take place.

Researchers analyzed language and found there are more emotional words that are negative. One study found that 62% of the emotional words were negative and 32% were positive. 74% of the total words in the English language describe personality traits as negative.

*Source: Wikipedia.*

Unfortunately, our brains have a negativity bias, and we tend to focus more on what's wrong rather than what's right. That's why it's important to repeat and emphasise positive messages more often.

Unless you attune yourself to the pitfalls of negativity, both as a provider of feedback and as a receiver, you easily trigger defensiveness. Instead of delivering messages intended to help correct behaviours, people will not be able to hear you.

So that they don't become counterproductive by overemphasising what's wrong, leaders should take heed when delivering feedback. Yet it's also important to be candid. Once again, trust is a big factor that paves the way.

## How to Give Feedback

There are many guidelines for giving feedback. Here is a concise one from an article published on Forbes.com on "How to Give Feedback that Works." Use this five-step model for feedback:

1. **Ask for permission to give feedback:** You'd be surprised how much of a difference this makes. A simple, "Hey, do you have a minute for some quick feedback?" can help the receiver of feedback be mentally ready for it, be it positive or negative.

2. **State what you observed:** Where possible, use specific examples and avoid being judgemental. "You don't give off a lot of energy in meetings" is not as helpful as, "In the meeting with Tina yesterday, I noticed that you didn't look at her when she spoke and didn't ask any questions."

3. **Explain the impact:** Point out the direct impact that resulted from this behaviour, again trying to be as specific as possible. Saying, "When you said X, it made me feel upset," or "I noticed that the customer became more irate" is much more effective

than "When you say X, you sound stupid." It's much more difficult to argue with "it made me feel," "I noticed that," or "I think that...," and using those phrases will keep the feedback session from devolving into a debate.

4. **Pause and ask for the other person's reaction:** Give them time to think through what you've said and react to it.

5. **Suggest concrete next steps:** Give one or two actionable suggestions that the other person can take in the future, to change this behaviour. They will appreciate that you are giving them the first step to improving the situation.

### TRY FEEDFORWARD INSTEAD OF FEEDBACK

Providing feedback has long been considered to be an essential skill for leaders. As they strive to achieve the goals of the organisation, employees need to know how they are doing. They need to know if their performance is in line with what their leaders expect. They need to learn what they have done well and what they need to change.

Traditionally, this information has been communicated in the form of "downward feedback" from leaders to their employees. Just as employees need feedback from leaders, leaders can benefit from feedback from their employees. Employees can provide useful input on the effectiveness of procedures and processes and as well as input to managers on their leadership effectiveness. This "upward feedback" has become increasingly common with the advent of 360° multi-rater assessments.

## TRY FEEDFORWARD INSTEAD OF FEEDBACK *(continued)*

But there is a fundamental problem with all types of feedback: it focuses on a past, on what has already occurred—not on the infinite variety of opportunities that can happen in the future. As such, feedback can be limited and static, as opposed to expansive and dynamic.

Feedforward asks for two suggestions for the future that might help someone achieve a positive change in their selected behaviour.

*We can change the future. We can't change the past.*
Feedforward helps people envision and focus on a positive future, not a failed past.

*It can be more productive to help people be "right," than prove they were "wrong."*

*(Source: The term feedforward was coined in a discussion that Marshall Goldsmith had with Jon Katzenbach, author of The Wisdom of Teams, Real Change Leaders and Peak Performance. For more information visit http://www.marshallgoldsmithfeedforward.com/html/Articles.htm.)*

# Pulling It Together:
# Three Guiding Principles to
# Accountability Leadership

In this chapter I've revealed that accountability comes through clarity of leadership communications, creating compelling consequences that work to bring about the right results, and conversations based in reality that drive a culture of responsibility. Let's review:

1. **Clear communications.** The keys to creating accountability throughout the organisation are embedded in the many ways leaders communicate. Leaders can never over-deliver their core messages. The more frequently they repeat the business core values, mission and strategies, the less confusion and ambiguity.

   The more specific you can be, through giving examples and telling stories, the better. Especially when it comes to values and ethics, there are many ways to interpret situations. Unless you spell out how values need to be applied on the job, people will make their own interpretations. Be clear on how you want people to apply rules and regulations and company values. Give them "if/then" scenarios.

   Leaders are required to communicate both the big picture and how that translates to goals and actions that will bring out intended business results. Above all, leaders must never lose sight of communicating why their employees' work matters to the company, the customers, and the community.

To meet their responsibilities to their followers, leaders are accountable for building and communicating:

1. Clarity of purpose and passion
2. Recognition and praise
3. Trust
4. Feedback that works

2. **Compelling consequences.** Accountable leaders are clear about laying out the consequences, both for errors and success. They create mechanisms for tolerating risks and mistakes. They know the importance of recognising and celebrating progress along the way.

   Leaders who practice accountability do not encourage finger pointing and blame. Instead they promote problem solving and creative thinking. Almost anyone can fall into the success delusion: that you're responsible for wins, and others are to blame for failures.

   Don't let this happen to you as a leader. Accountable leadership requires stellar behaviours that others can observe and copy. Instead of asking, "Who did this?" ask your people, "What needs to be done now?"

3. **Conversations that build an accountability culture.** The conversations you have with your people are the foundations to an accountability culture. Every conversation you have either builds trust or chips it away.

   As a leader you are responsible for focusing on the positive signs of progress while not ignoring the need for change. Your sensitivity to fairness is crucial if you to want to understand how people work together and you want to inspire them to do their best.

I don't know any leader who doesn't struggle with giving effective feedback. Accountability leadership requires high levels of competency in having productive feedback and feedforward conversations, as well as teaching others throughout the organisation the skills of the language of accountability.

In the next chapter, we will review motivational theory and look at what really works.

# Checklist for the
# Three Guiding Principles

Ask yourself regularly:

**A. Clear messages:**

- ☑ Am I communicating clearly, reminding myself and others of our overarching mission, values and strategy?

- ☑ Do I relate the big picture to real world situations, people, and business realities?

- ☑ Am I connecting the dots to small daily tasks and goals?

- ☑ Do I repeat messages clearly and simply?

- ☑ Am I generous with recognition and praise?

**B. Consequences:**

- ☑ Do I have compelling consequences in place that encourage people to use their strengths and creativity?

- ☑ Do I discourage behaviours that distract while encouraging fun and friendships?

- ☑ Do I encourage problem solving in new ways?

- ☑ Do I let people come up with their own ideas?

- ☑ Do I recognise achievements personally?

## C. Conversations

☑ Am I receptive to conversations that reveal realities I may not see or even like?

☑ Do I give feedback in a manner that can be received? Do I use feedforward?

☑ Do I focus on behaviours without being judgemental?

☑ Do I allow people the chance to express themselves without interrupting them with my solutions?

☑ Do I act like I'm open to hearing about mistakes and other opinions?

☑ Do my conversations build trust?

# Chapter 2

# The Science of Motivation

*When people are motivated by inspiration, to a cause
greater than themselves, their behaviour is deeply
personal. They are committed and engaged to help and
participate, even at personal sacrifice.*

Simon Sinek,
*Start with Why: How Great Leaders Inspire Others to Act*

**A**ccountability works, but only if you create the right conditions
for your people in your business.

There is no lack of business books that proclaim the secret solutions
to this problem. Many of the leading business books have value
in this respect and contribute pieces of the puzzle of how to ignite
motivation through accountability leadership.

But after putting these books down, it's often difficult to retain or explain their essence. Many of them are written by experienced consultants using acronyms and branded terminology.

Who remembers, for example, specifically how these branded methods work?

- In-the-box, out-of-the-box thinking (Leadership Self-Deception)
- Above the line, below the line experiences (Oz Principle)
- Level 5 Leadership (From Good to Great)

When there are too many pieces of a puzzle, too much good advice, you have to work hard to wrap your mind around what to do for your own situation.

What does it mean to build a culture of accountability for your own people, in your business? What are your first steps towards an Accountability Plan, in plain English?

## Incentive Plans Don't Work

Most managers believe in the power of rewards such as cash bonuses and perks. The vast majority of global corporations use programs intended to motivate employees by tying compensation to a performance index.

What's surprising is the lack of doubt about that assumption: that people will do a better job if promised an incentive. It's simply assumed to be true. Yet we've known for some time that rewards alone do not create a lasting commitment.

Punishments and rewards are very similar: each has a temporary effect because they're manipulative. Rewards change what people do in the short term. Do rewards motivate people? Yes, they motivate people to get rewards.

This is not without a cost. The number one casualty of rewards is creativity. People will focus on doing what's necessary to win, not on the purpose of the work itself.

Incentive plans in and of themselves do not comprise an effective Accountability Plan. In fact, research indicates that a pay-for-performance system tends to make people fear failure and become less enthusiastic about their work and less likely to approach it with a commitment to excellence.

Numerous studies in laboratories and workplaces have shown that rewards typically undermine the very processes they are intended to enhance. We know this; we've had evidence since the early studies of Edward Deci in the 1970s showed the importance of intrinsic motivation as opposed to extrinsic rewards. (Deci, E.L., Intrinsic Motivation, Plenum Publishing 1975.)

Numerous studies since then have confirmed how external rewards interfere with igniting passion, energy and innovative ideas. Yet we continue to reward performance with bonuses and perks.

We're convinced this is simply common sense and should work. We don't ignore that intrinsic motivation reigns supreme, but in the face of confusion about how exactly to reach the hearts and minds of each employee, we cover our bases with rewards programs anyway.

## Can You Spot the Lack of Accountability?

While many leaders and organisations claim to recognise the urgent need for greater accountability, it's elusive. Few leaders know how to obtain it or maintain it.

Leaders are generally quite good at workarounds that mask the symptoms of poor accountability. Perhaps an organisation has an excess of emergencies which attract the knights in shining armour to come riding in on white chargers to save the day. This is a sure sign that systems and policies of accountability are not in place or not used.

Maybe an organisation has the same people who consistently remain late at work to cover the shortcomings of others, or fail to give others the opportunity to perform at their best for lack of trust or unwillingness to share credit.

Even with these workarounds for poor accountability, if you scratch just below the surface, the typical signs of poor accountability can be seen in the volume of excuses and blaming that people engage in. In all workplaces, there is a vast library of creative excuses why work isn't getting done.

- I don't have enough time.
- If only we had adequate staff (resources, etc.).
- The schedule is impossible to meet.
- That's not my job.
- I don't know how, anyway the boss didn't say that.
- The staff can't be trusted / are incompetent.

- It's the _____ (competition, the economy, government regulations—fill in your blank).

Whatever the justification for failure to complete a task, instead of focusing on why it can't be done or wasn't done, turn your attention to "what else can we do?" Whenever people blame other people, places and things, you have an accountability problem.

## An Accountability Attitude

To be fair, there are valid obstacles in all projects. Everyone at one time or another succumbs to an excuse to get off the hook. But that doesn't work well for solving whatever problems face the organisation, its leaders, and everyone who works in the company.

Shortfalls and failures occur all the time. It's a natural part of business and life. Attempting to duck responsibility only serves to prolong suffering, delay correction—and worse—*prevents learning from mistakes.*

Acceptance of greater accountability for results can get a person, a team, and the organisation back on the path to success. This requires adopting an attitude of accountability. Performance invariably improves when people take on accountability and ownership for results.

Actually, in my experience, people want to be accountable—but they don't always know it. Accountability systems are empowering. Being empowered to produce better results provides more meaning to their work, and brings them a boatload of satisfaction.

*An attitude of accountability lies at the core of any effort to improve quality, satisfy customers, empower people, build teams, create new products, maximise effectiveness and get results.*

The Oz Principle, by Roger Connors, Tom Smith, and Craig Hickman (Portfolio, 2004).

## Missing: How to Inspire Accountability

While researching leadership accountability, I found a lot of good rhetoric about how important accountability is. Few would disagree with this.

But you can't get there by telling people this. You can't announce your new "Accountability Plan" and expect people to jump on board. Why? Because you can't tell people how to feel. They have to want it.

- Unless they really trust you, you can't tell people how much better their jobs would be if only they would adopt your exciting new Accountability Plan.

- You can't tell hard-working people to begin Monday morning to "see it, own it, solve it and just do it."

- It's an even bigger challenge to inspire the slackers and those who are disengaged to get with the program.

There are ample "reasons why" to improve accountability. I don't see enough information on "how" to make it happen.

Let's review a few background theories that have been proven to work for motivating workers. This leads us all the way back to the same issues managers have struggled with since the Hawthorne studies of the early 1930s.

## THE HAWTHORNE STUDIES

In the late 20s and early 30s, management set out to understand the effect of lighting on the productivity of factory workers at the Hawthorne plant for Western Electric.

What they found was surprising: the variable for productivity was not the amount of light. It was the degree of social interaction the workers experienced because they were being studied.

In other words, paying attention to their work conditions created conditions for improved productivity, as did increasing the social interactions between workers. Yet at the time, most managers chose to ignore this fact; instead, bosses continued to favour control and command techniques based on time studies for improved performance.

## How Do You Motivate Employees?

In the 1960s, psychologist Frederick Herzberg contributed greatly to managerial understanding of what motivates workers. He found that one of the greatest motivators at work is *our need for achievement and recognition.*

After more than fifty years, for new generations of employees, this need remains unmet, causing a loss of natural motivation. The problem is compounded when what's perceived as interesting and challenging work becomes routine with time and repetition.

When this happens, management often resorts to incentive plans and bonuses. While rewards may work temporarily, it often motivates people to game the system and focus on the reward itself. It squelches innovation and takes the focus away from doing the right things the right way.

One of the best ways to motivate staff is to make their jobs more enriching. You can do this by providing opportunities for growth and education that lead to a sense of mastery and achievement. Yet training programs are too often cut back.

Consequently, many jobs become routine, like running on a treadmill. A lot of energy is spent, but unless management pays attention to workers when they achieve milestones, growth and progress, energy eventually fizzles out.

### FREDERICK HERZBERG

Frederick Irving Herzberg (1923—2000) was an American psychologist who became one of the most influential names in business management.

He is most famous for introducing job enrichment and the Motivator-Hygiene theory.

His 1968 publication "One More Time, How Do You Motivate Employees?" had sold 1.2 million reprints by 1987 and was the most requested article from the *Harvard Business Review*.

## The Carrot and Stick Theory

In the Harvard Business Review, one of the bestselling articles of all time is Frederick Herzberg's *"Once Again, How Do You Motivate People?"* (HBR, September/October 1987).

In it, he distinguishes between intrinsic and extrinsic motivators. In the work place, extrinsic motivation is known as "carrots and sticks." Carrots and sticks are everywhere. They are so woven into the cultures of most workplaces we hardly notice them. If you meet a quota, you get a bonus. If you miss a deadline, you don't get a privilege.

While carrots and sticks do motivate people, they have some serious flaws. First and foremost, they're not self-sustaining. If you remove the reward or the punishment, the desired behaviour stops or reduces. People ask, "Why do that if they no longer reward it?"

External rewards place an enormous burden on managers to continually provide a steady diet of fresh carrots and bigger sticks in order to keep people motivated.

Extrinsic motivation is shortsighted. Furthermore, it doesn't bring out the best in your employees.

As for productivity, at least two dozen studies over the last three decades have conclusively shown that people who expect to receive a reward for completing a task simply do not perform as well as those who expect no reward at all. Worse, they misplace their focus on getting the prize instead of doing great work.

Managers often use incentive systems as a substitute for giving workers what they really need to do a good job. Treating workers well—by providing useful feedback, social support, and the room for self-determination—is the essence of good management.

Offering a bonus and waiting for results requires much less thought and effort on the part of leaders.

## Motivation Is an Inside Job

Intrinsic motivation is far more powerful because it comes from within. It is self-generating, self-sustaining, and pleasurable. With personal motivation we do a task for the enjoyment of doing it. It triggers the brain to release dopamine, the neurochemical involved in rewards and feeling good.

Intrinsic motivation is what pulls you to act on your own volition regardless of what anyone else thinks or does. The reward is doing the task itself. When people are intrinsically motivated they will work longer and harder, be more creative, and use more flexible thinking in problem solving.

In order to truly motivate people, managers need to tap into the intrinsic motivators within employees. That's why as leaders, we need to learn more about the inner work life of people. How can we reach the hearts and minds of people to bring out their best?

## Creating Flow Conditions

Mihaly Csikszentmihalyi (pronounced "chick-sent-mee-high") has studied motivation in people when they're engaged in optimal work experiences. We've come to know such moments as "flow," and it's similar to athletes being "in the zone."

Flow happens when people are so engaged in activities they lose themselves. It's a highly self-motivated state typified by total absorption in the task, single-minded immersion, and spontaneous joy.

How do you get your employees into this highly engaged state? You cannot force them, nor can you command them. Yet there are certain conditions that set the stage for flow experiences to happen.

As a manager you have a lot of influence over creating these optimal conditions. This is important because flow provides the fuel for motivation. You don't have to work hard to engage people when it happens.

In order for flow states to arise, you need the following conditions:

1. Clear goals and expectations (as we talked about in Chapter 1).

2. Optimally challenging goals that stretch one to bring out their best work.

3. Immediate and consistent feedback and recognition of progress.

One of the ways to ensure optimally challenging work is to involve people in setting their goals. This helps them to feel a sense of ownership but also to find the critical balance between hard and not too hard.

## HOW "FLOW" LINKS WITH ACCOUNTABILITY

What's interesting about the three conditions necessary for flow experiences to occur is that they are very similar to what I've suggested as optimal conditions for accountability:

1. Clear leadership communication
2. Compelling consequences
3. Conversations that promote a culture of accountability through healthy feedback on progress.

How perfectly ideal that would be if, as a consequence of setting up accountability in your organisation, you inadvertently produced flow experiences as people went about their work.

## Autonomy

Being in control and having choices is an important aspect of life. Everyone needs to feel self-directing, even when complying with job requirements and regulations. When anyone tries to exert control over us, even when it's in our best interests, there's a part of us that wants to rebel.

That's why it becomes essential for managers to pay attention to how accountability can backfire. Anything you can do to help employees enjoy a greater sense of freedom and control at work will increase their level of motivation.

Giving autonomy to workers is the opposite of command and control management. And yet, too much freedom, too many choices and lack of direction and consequences are elements that are just as bad for people who seek job satisfaction. The key lies in crafting compelling consequences that resonate with workers. That is what we'll cover in Chapter 3.

# Pulling It Together

This chapter reviewed some of the main theories about how managers motivate people for greater engagement in their jobs. You'll need to be aware of these concepts as you decide what kind of accountability plan will work for your people in your organisation.

In Chapter 1, I suggest that leaders are ultimately responsible for creating accountability throughout the organisation. How they handle mistakes, blame, accountability, and credit goes a long way to setting the stage for accountability.

Most importantly for leaders, what they say and do matters. Leaders can't get others to give their best if they aren't sincere and congruent with their own actions and words. They may set up accountability systems and processes, but they will fail unless the foundations of trust are solid.

Trust is established each time a leader communicates with people. That is why clear and concise messages are a keystone element to an accountability program that works.

In this chapter, I reviewed what we now understand are the basics of motivating people at work. Carrots and sticks have their limits; tapping into the internal energy of people works better. Ideally, people work best when they experience "flow" conditions. People want to feel in control of their work.

However, even good routines become boring after a while. Keeping jobs interesting and challenging requires managers' help. In our next chapter, we address compelling consequences that work in creating effective accountability programs.

# CHAPTER 3

# Compelling Consequences

*"Your greatest source of power for creating compelling consequences is your ability to change how people feel."*

Jeff Grimshaw and Gregg Baron,
*Leadership without Excuses*, McGraw-Hill, 2010.

How do you create high accountability in other people through compelling consequences?

I've seen first-hand how smart leaders harness their power to influence feelings in people in order to bring about high accountability and performance. It works.

And, it's not as difficult as it may seem. Yet many leaders are still focusing on external rewards and incentives. They're not using this powerful option. As a leader, you have enormous capacity to tap into people's internal drives and motivations by changing how they feel.

In 2002 Daniel Kahneman and Amos Tversky won the Nobel Prize in economics for their work in decision-making and consumer choices. One of their breakthrough ideas was that people don't conform to the logic of traditional economics, which for 275 years has discounted the importance of emotion and feelings in economic decision making.

Kahneman writes, "Utility cannot be divorced from emotion ... A theory of choice that completely ignores feelings ... leads to prescriptions that do not maximise the utility of outcomes as they are actually experienced."

As an example, your top performer chooses to stick with you over another job offer with more money because of the way her current job makes her feel. She may feel respected, appreciated, purposeful, autonomous, valued, and recognised. Or some combination of other feelings.

People don't make rational decisions based on simple monetary or other objective criterion. They always consider how they feel. This seems obvious, yet it's taken economists and business experts a long time to recognise it. There's now a new branch of economics called behavioural economics that studies how feelings and emotions impact our decisions.

In other words, most of the time we decide what to do based not on objective calculations of benefits and utility, but on how it actually makes us feel.

Let's return to our challenge of how to create consequences that tap into this "new" information.

## List Your Consequence Capital

In *Leading without Excuses*, authors Grimshaw and Baron use the term "consequence capital," for capturing the essence of this powerful motivator. Like your other assets, your ability to use consequences effectively is indeed valuable. Here is a great suggestion from their book on how to fully realise the value of your consequence capital.

First, make a list of all the ways you currently motivate and incentivise your people when you want to get them to do something new or different. Write down all the consequences you know of— both positive and negative—that you use to motivate people. Your list probably includes things like these:

- Compensation
- Bonuses
- "Thanks"
- Time off
- Status/title
- Privileges (parking, dining, working remotely, flex time, etc.)
- Operational resources (people, budget, etc.)
- Admin support (mentor, executive coach)
- Termination of service
- Loss of a privilege
- Scheduling preferences and/or loss of preference

You'll probably think of more as we go along. Now think about losing a valuable employee, one of your stars. What would she say would be the reasons she would never accept a job offer at higher pay? What are the emotions you imagine would be on her list of reasons to stay?

Now make a list of all the ways you could influence or change the way someone feels about their job. Usually, when I challenge leaders to make such a list, they start coming up with all sorts of "emotional" rewards, like these:

- Acceptance
- Public recognition, credit
- Responsiveness to requests
- Time and attention
- Inclusion in decisions and activities
- Privileges including information
- Familiarity
- Acknowledgment in public, with peers, with superiors
- Consultation, seek advice and feedback
- Third-party compliments, spreading a positive story
- Partnering with them
- Staying out of their way
- Introductions
- Visibility
- Conveniences
- Free time
- Freedom to fail, experiment
- Absolution for past errors
- New experiences, tasks

As a leader, you have more options for compelling consequences than you realise. You have tremendous capacity to change the way people feel. There are so many ways you can tap into people's emotions and feelings without being intrusive or inappropriate.

## What *Really* Motivates Your People?

Give this some serious thought. One great way to tap into this is by having conversations with a few of your people. Ask them what makes them feel good at work. They'll probably give you more good ideas that work for motivating them.

What are the things you want to encourage more of? Match these tasks up with appropriate rewards. What are the things you no longer want to tolerate?

You can use this same list to discourage behaviours that are not aligned with the organisation's culture and goals. By taking positive consequences away from people, you create negative consequences. You discourage misaligned behaviours because people don't like the way it feels to be excluded from the privileges and recognition that others get.

There are a few things to keep in mind when using "emotional" rewards.

- **Value is relative.** What one person feels good about depends on his or her expectations.

- **Value is compared.** People make social comparisons and are sensitive to fairness.

- **People are sensitive to** principles of fairness and rewards for nonperformers.

- **People get accustomed to** a reward after time and it loses its perceived value.

You may be perceived as rewarding non-performers when you give them additional time and attention. You also commit a gross "unfairness error" when you fail to take away a privilege, thereby tolerating their misaligned behaviour.

## The Fairness Principle

Most people are sensitive to what's fair. If you stop challenging someone because of their incompetence, you are, in one sense, rewarding them. If you spend additional time with them, which is something perceived as valuable, you are also seen as rewarding them.

By the same hand, when you give extra work to your star performers, you can be perceived as unfairly distributing the work load. However, when the tasks you are assigning are desired because of their value as challenging goals, you contribute to a person's growth and development.

You can see the fine line here between what is perceived as a reward or a punishment. It all depends on context and what your employee values. You can't know this without asking them and having the conversation.

In other words, you can't assume that what you *perceive* as a privilege is *received* as such by the person you're trying to motivate.

I'm a big fan of using new experiences and challenges as a reward for high performers. The more unique or novel an experience, the better it works as a developmental opportunity. But unless you've checked with your employee, you can't be sure how it is perceived. This requires discussion. You can't tell someone how they're supposed to feel. You have to ask them about their perceptions.

## Loss Aversion

One other point from Kahneman and the behavioural economists is that people are twice as sensitive to a loss as they are to a gain. Loss aversion affects everyone in life and work choices. As a manager, this is good to know, because taking away a privilege or a task can be a powerful negative consequence.

However, you can also administer a negative consequence unintentionally. Whenever you change your mind about task assignments, or forget someone, you're creating a loss that can be perceived as a negative consequence. It's not without reverberations.

On the other hand, this also means you now have more options and consequences for poor performers. You aren't limited to delivering a warning or firing them.

- You can withdraw assignments, information, autonomy, and attention.

- You can start limiting your time with them.

- You can restrict access to resources including the Internet until you get compliance.

These actions must be applied with openness and transparency, lest you fall into the trap of failing to take responsibility for your actions.

## Consequence Timing

Small and frequent feedback improves well-being more than massive rewards at a distant date. People prefer smaller rewards (your attention, your comments) to larger payoffs later on (an annual performance review or prize at a yearly banquet).

To get the greatest motivational value, bring your consequences close to the actual performance. Even as important as timeliness is specificity. Tell your people exactly what they did that made a difference. Tell them personally, and also in a way that others hear about it too. Be clear on the benefits their actions bring to the group and to the organisation.

## Positive vs. Negative Feedback

We've known for a few decades that positive feedback is far more motivating than negative. Yet managers who give criticism sandwiched between two positive comments wonder why it often provokes negative defensiveness and excuses. This is because our brains have a negative bias, and we tend to remember negative comments more acutely.

And if criticism is sandwiched between a couple of nice comments, we feel manipulated.

For example, you're impressed with one of your staff and want to reinforce his good work. You approach him after a large presentation and say:

> *"That was a great presentation, Dale. Next time, don't forget to include the Acme data. I thought we discussed that. Other than that, it was very effective, nice work."*

Dale only hears how his boss was disappointed in him and wants to defend his decision. He doesn't learn a thing, and he now wants to convince his boss he was right. He doesn't even hear the boss's compliment because it was non-specific and vague. Their interaction becomes tinged with negativity, while ironically the boss believes he was giving good feedback.

People need to know they're valued and become more receptive to your feedback when it is reinforced by a majority of positive comments.

## Positivity in Action: The Progress Principle

What's the best way to ensure a majority of positive feedback in a normal working environment without being insincere or contrived? Let's face it—what's most noticeable is *what's wrong and what's not working*. The key lies in focusing on progress, not perfection.

In a remarkable study, two researchers asked people to keep track of their inner working lives by writing down their thoughts on a daily basis to see how interactions with managers and colleagues affected them at work.

In *The Progress Principle: Using Small Wins to Ignite Joy, Engagement, and Creativity at Work* (Harvard Business Press, 2011), Teresa Amabile and Steven Kramer describe how people with great inner work lives have:

- Consistently positive emotions.
- Strong motivation.
- Favourable perceptions of the organisation, their work and their colleagues.

The worst managers undermine others' inner work lives, often unwittingly. Through rigorous analysis of nearly 12,000 diary entries provided by 238 employees at seven companies, Amabile and Kramer found surprising results on the factors that affect performance.

What matters most is forward momentum in meaningful work—in a word, progress. Managers who recognise the need for even small wins set the stage for high performance.

But surveys of CEOs and project leaders reveal that ninety-five percent fundamentally misunderstand the need for this critical motivator.

## HOW TO FACILITATE PROGRESS

There are three events that occur in the workplace that can undermine people's inner work lives:

1. **Setbacks**—The biggest downer, yet inevitable in any sort of meaningful work
2. **Inhibitors**—Events that directly hinder project work
3. **Toxins**—Interpersonal events that undermine the people doing the work

As a leader, it is vitally important to counteract negative events such as these by focusing on the positive perceptions associated with small wins and progress, enabling your employees to experience the energy and drive that fuels high performance.

There are two key forces that enable progress:

1. **Catalysts**—Events that directly advance project work, such as:
   a. Clear goals
   b. Autonomy
   c. Resources, including time
   d. Reviewing lessons from errors and success
   e. Free flow of ideas

2. **Nourishers**—Interpersonal events that uplift workers, including:
   a. Encouragement and support
   b. Demonstrations of respect
   c. Collegiality

## How Managers Get It Wrong

In a survey by Amabile and Kramer, 669 managers ranked five factors that influence motivation and emotions at work:

1. Recognition
2. Incentives
3. Interpersonal support
4. Clear goals
5. Support for making progress in the work

Managers incorrectly ranked "support for making progress" dead last, with most citing "recognition for good work" as the most important motivator.

Research shows that those managers who recognise and celebrate small wins are those who bring out the best in their people. The ability to focus on progress is paramount.

Negative events carry a greater impact than positive ones. We pay more attention to them, remember them, and spend more time thinking and talking about them.

That's why it's so important for managers and team leaders to counteract negative events with positive perceptions and comments.

The way to motivate your team the most is to facilitate their progress by recognising small wins. This is the key principle revealed by rigorous analysis of daily journal entries by Teresa Amabile and Steven Kramer in *The Progress Principle*.

After sifting through pages of daily entries about events at work, Kramer and Amabile realised that everyday events affect the inner work life of both staff and managers. As a leader, you help when you tend to your people by supporting them and their progress along the way. People perform best when their thoughts are positive and strong.

At the end of the day, review the day's events and the work goals that were actually achieved. No matter how difficult and disappointing, no matter how small the accomplishments, you will benefit by focusing on what you have been able to do. Setbacks are inevitable, but they can be learning opportunities.

Management responsibilities can take a particular toll on day-by-day perceptions, emotions, and motivations. The single type of event that most frequently triggers a positive inner work life experience is progress.

To boost your own inner work life as a manager, be sure to provide your people with catalysts and nourishers, and buffer them from inhibitors and toxins as much as possible. That way you'll make progress in your own managerial work and set up a positive progress loop.

## THE LEADERSHIP TRUST DEFICIT

Only seven percent of employees say they trust their senior leaders to look out for their best interests. In a 2011 Maritz survey, more than 90,000 employees worldwide said the No. 1 driver of employee engagement was "when senior management takes a genuine interest in me as an individual."

Employees want consistency between their leaders' words and actions. But only 11 percent of employees strongly agree that their managers "walk the talk," the Maritz poll reveals.

Fairly or unfairly, leaders' behaviours are magnified and weighted, including their values, work ethics, integrity and perceived honesty. Employees have high moral expectations for those they choose to follow.

Why do almost 90 percent of leaders rate so poorly on measures of trust? Roughly half of all managers don't trust their leaders, according to a survey of 450 executives at 30 global companies by Dr Robert Hurley, author of *The Decision to Trust (2012)*.

These statistics are troubling, as distrustful environment creates expensive—and sometimes irreparable—problems.

A Watson Wyatt Worldwide study of 12,750 U.S. workers in all major industries found that companies with high trust levels outperform their low-trust counterparts by 186 percent.

## Everybody's Different

Everybody is motivated—just not by the same things. Your task as manager is to find out what drives your people. You need to have conversations that explore their needs.

Each person does what they do for their own reasons. They don't do things for your reasons. As leader, you have to understand what is motivating your people so you can show them how the things you want them to do are in their own best interest.

## Without Trust Nothing Works

Why do nine out of ten leaders rate so poorly on measures of trust? Whether you're actually trustworthy or not, it doesn't take much to create an atmosphere of distrust. But the solutions aren't as complicated as one might think.

To improve your connection to your people and build trust, try these techniques:

1. **Go on a walk around.** Walk around the office each day to touch base with individual contributors to your company's success. While email and group meetings are important, one-on-one "face time" is critical.

2. **Capture vital statistics.** Learn about each employee's life: spouse's name, children's names and ages, major hobbies. Use questions to elicit meaningful information: "Where are you from?" or "What do you do on your days off?"

3. **Find what drives them.** Instead of focusing on differences, find mutual interests (hobbies, desires, career goals). Explore each person's guiding motivations.

4. **Ask for ideas and feedback:** Trust must already be established for people to be honest with you. Ask what they need to perform their jobs better. Acknowledge that you hear their opinions and will think about what they've said. Don't dismiss or argue the merits of their input; offer a simple and genuine "thanks for sharing that."

Acknowledge progress and milestones: In many organisations, problems are solved, barriers are surmounted, tasks are completed... and nothing is noted. People crave acknowledgment and recognition, so seize these opportunities to build trust. Celebrate progress. Don't let it slip by unnoticed.

## Anxiety and Confidence

Often something as simple as helping build up a person's confidence goes a long way towards creating accountability and performance. People need to feel you care and believe in them.

Become aware of your people's emotional experiences, and when they feel anxious, share with them your stories and similar experiences. You can do a lot to relieve their doubts and boost their performance.

Everyone wants to make their numbers and deliver results, and even more so when they know doing so will bring them acceptance, recognition, and rewards. But mostly they want to feel less anxious and more confident about their work.

People want to feel confident about their jobs, to be able to handle unexpected events, and trust the reliability of the systems and processes they use. They don't want to lose their autonomy to people who don't understand their needs. They also don't want to look like idiots.

When you boost their confidence and reduce anxiety you help them do their jobs better. Here are a few suggestions:

- Relationships build confidence. Make sure your people have opportunities for social activities and making connections.

- Speak the language of "we." There's a reason we work in teams.

- Treat all people with respect, focusing on their behaviours, not personalities.

# Pulling It Together

In Chapter 1, I suggested that leaders are ultimately responsible for creating accountability throughout the organisation. How they handle mistakes, blame, accountability, and credit goes a long way to achieving positive results.

Most importantly for leaders, what they say matters. Leaders can't get others to give their best if they aren't sincere and their message isn't congruent with their own actions and words. They set up accountability systems and processes, but none of them will work unless trust is solid.

In Chapter 2, we reviewed some of the main theories about how managers motivate people for greater engagement in their jobs. We also discussed why some incentive and pay-for-performance programs either don't work at all or yield the wrong results. You'll need to be aware of these concepts as you decide what kind of accountability plan will work for your people in your organisation.

The science of motivation in Chapter 2 was an important precursor to Chapter 3, in which we examined how consequences work in motivating high accountability and performance in other people. How can you set up processes so that a consequence is motivating for the right results?

How can you discourage non-aligned performance? What obstacles and barriers are common?

Next, in Chapter 4, we'll address the issues of creating a culture of accountability fuelled by intention, driven by the power of conversation, and sustained by organisational systems and design.

# Checklist for
# Compelling Consequences

Ask yourself these questions about the consequences you use:

- ☑ Am I communicating clear messages about desired goals and results, both for the organisation and for our team?

- ☑ Do my people know what's at stake for the organisation?

- ☑ Do my people know why their jobs matter?

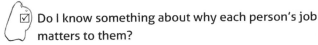 ☑ Do I know something about why each person's job matters to them?

- ☑ Do people understand the meaning of their work to the organisation, to their team, and to them personally?

- ☑ Do I offer clear goals that encourage people to use their strengths and creativity?

- ☑ Do I discourage behaviours that distract them from their goals?

- ☑ Do I encourage fun and friendships?

- ☑ Do I encourage problem solving in new ways?

- ☑ Do I let people come up with their own ideas?

- ☑ Am I accepting of mistakes, and do I work on turning them into learning opportunities?

- ☑ Do I recognise achievements personally and immediately?

☑ Do I signal what specific benefits to the organisation their actions have brought?

☑ Am I providing clear negative consequences for bad behaviour?

☑ Do I avoid unintentionally reinforcing poor performance?

☑ Do I take advantage of loss aversion to motivate poor performers?

☑ Do I follow up with people regularly, offering attention for small wins and progress?

# CHAPTER 4

# Creating a Culture of Accountability

*Where does accountability start? It starts with you, as soon as you open your mouth for the purpose of voicing a word.*

Mihnea Moldoveanu,
*"The Promise: The Basic Building Block of Accountability"*
(Rotman Magazine Fall 2009)

In an ideal high performing organisation, there is a natural flow of responsibility and accountability. Organisational culture and systems compel members to step up and take personal responsibility for their own outcomes while holding one another accountable for the delivery of their promises. Leaders set the tone for how to speak and act. Managers follow suit and teach personal responsibility and accountability to front line staff. Individuals at all levels step up to the plate.

If accountability is going to take hold and thrive, it needs to happen throughout an organisation on a cultural level. It's an easy thing to preach accountability by admonishing everyone to "own" the organisation's problems. "But if that's not accompanied by a systematic effort to create conditions of accountability at the institutional level, even your very best people are going to find it challenging to translate those rather empty words into action," write authors Jeff Grimshaw and Gregg Baron in *Leadership without Excuses: How to Create Accountability and High Performance* (McGraw Hill, 2010).

Implementing stronger performance management systems is a typical response by organisations to increase culture-wide accountability. Yet performance management as a system will fail if people aren't intrinsically motivated.

How do you get people to bring their best efforts to the table? How do leaders instill a culture of accountability? Certainly, there needs to be a system to measure progress. Yet with many accountability programs, the best intentions inadvertently create pitfalls that are counterproductive to getting desired business results.

Sustaining a culture of accountability throughout an organisation requires not only processes and measures, but a high level of skilled communication for feedback and performance reviews. Without that, feedback is perceived as negative, and is discouraging rather than motivating.

We discussed how important communication skills are for leaders and people in positions of responsibility in Chapter 1. It's also important to teach those skills to everyone in the organisation so that they can speak the *language of accountability* to peers and teams without encountering defensiveness.

## Pitfalls on the Road to an Accountability Culture

Here are a few alerts from Leadership Without Excuses about the obstacles leaders face trying to improve accountability in their organisational culture.

1. **Measurements.** When you use numbers and charts to track goals and tasks, you make expectations clear. You can align consequences with performance. However, as authors Grimshaw and Baron point out, sometimes what's easy to measure isn't what's important to measure. This pitfall occurs when leaders place unwarranted faith in numbers. This is because many people confuse correlation with causality and underestimate the effects of variables and randomness.

   For a refresher course on this, read Nassim Taleb's *Fooled by Randomness* and Phil Rosezweig's *Halo Effect*. I've included here in the following text box a summary of three common delusions about performance in organisations that often occurs when we misinterpret data.

   To quote Grimshaw and Baron, *"When your approach to measurement is dubious, you equip people to 1) take the results seriously when they are favorable but 2) discount them when they aren't."*

2. **Process and methodology.** Following a methodology or set process (Six Sigma, etc.) is usually good because it allows

people to get things done in a way that is predictable, stable, repeatable and efficient. But the pitfall occurs when you lose sight of the big picture, your company strategy, mission and values. When your results are compromised, then your process has become an obstacle instead of a guidepost.

3. **Results.** If you focus only on results, it's easy for people to achieve the ends by any means necessary. This opens the door to ethical, reputational, and legal obstacles. Business failure histories are rife with examples of goals gone awry. The truth is we live and work in complex environments where randomness and unusual circumstances can pop up at any time.

Employees can do all the things they're supposed to do and still not get the results you seek. Business often requires a nuanced perspective. Focusing only on results can inadvertently incentivise short-term thinking that jeopardises long-term goals and interests.

## PERFORMANCE DELUSIONS: MISINTERPRETING DATA

### Delusion #1: The Halo Effect

Psychologist Edward Thorndike researched the ways superiors rated subordinates during World War I. If a soldier was given a high rating for one trait, his superior officer usually provided high ratings for all other traits. And if a soldier was rated sub-par on a trait, he usually garnered low ratings for all other traits.

Thorndike called this the "Halo Effect": our tendency to make inferences about specific traits on the basis of a general impression. It's difficult for most people to measure discrete traits; we tend to blend them together. The Halo Effect tricks the mind into creating and maintaining a coherent, consistent picture.

When companies are profitable and sales are growing, we routinely attribute positive evaluations to other performance particulars. Numbers don't lie; we trust them. So, when we make inferences about company culture, customer outreach and core strategies based on financials, we succumb to the Halo Effect.

While the Halo Effect is not the only delusion that distorts our thinking about business, it's the most basic one. This flaw permeates most surveys and interviews, weakens the quality of data, and diminishes our ability to think clearly about important factors that lead to key decisions.

### Delusion #2: Correlation and Causation

To identify high performance, you must gather data using independent variables.

## PERFORMANCE DELUSIONS: MISINTERPRETING DATA *(continued)*

But even when rigorous research standards are applied, there's still a tendency to apply faulty reasoning. We continually infer *causality from correlation*. It's popular to assume that having satisfied employees leads to high performance, but this can be an erroneous assumption.

A more reliable statistic may be employee turnover. A low turnover rate may correlate with the numbers of employees who report job satisfaction.

The challenge is to untangle the direction of causality. Does lower employee turnover lead to higher company performance? Or does higher company performance lead to lower employee turnover? Pinpointing the distinction is critical to determining how much you should invest in achieving greater levels of satisfaction versus other objectives.

### Delusion #3: Single Explanation

Most studies look at a single explanation for performance and cast the others aside. The problem is that other factors—a strong company culture, customer focus or great leadership—are correlated.

This is why it's so difficult to identify what drives performance. Even if you avoid the Halo Effect, you must still consider alternative explanations. So many factors contribute to performance that it's hard to accurately differentiate between the various considerations.

I recently read about a consultant's experience with public transportation in Southeast Asia. He was waiting for a bus and noticed several empty vehicles, which passed by without stopping. After finally arriving by taxi to his appointment, he asked his host about the empty buses. It turns out the drivers have a schedule to meet and are rewarded for getting back on time. When they're behind schedule, they simply eliminate stops.

This illustrates how the best intentions can lead to the wrong results. And there are other obstacles to avoid on the way to establishing a culture of accountability.

## More Obstacles to Cultural Accountability

Besides being aware of the pitfalls of relying too much on measurements, processes, and results, there are other common blocks to accountability that you'll need to address to achieve a disciplined culture of accountability.

In a *Harvard Business Review* blog post, "Let's Bring Back Accountability," July 30, 2012, Deborah Mills-Scofield points out several obstacles:

- **Fear of the consequences of failure:** We've known for some time now that a culture that encourages creativity must allow for making mistakes and adjustments. When failure is punished, e.g. by poor performance appraisal, termination, loss of status or promotion, people stop trying. Accountability is crushed—along with creativity and innovation—when there is too much at stake for failing.

- **Fear of loss of control.** When people don't trust others in the organisation, they won't participate in an accountability plan that depends on others. They think, "I may not be in control of all the factors of success; my success depends on others who might not pull their weight; I fear other factors may arise to block my success that are out of my control..."

- **Lack of commitment on both sides.** This happens when the request isn't important enough to go to the top of the priority list or the requester doesn't follow through. Trade-offs always have to be made—which means sacrifice—of time, priorities, perhaps of the things we are passionate about. Accountability works both ways.

- **The rise of uncertainty.** It's difficult to accept responsibility for something when the outcome is less certain to predict. Success used to be more linear and defined. In today's business environment, the path to success is not always predictable, and the outcomes often less tangible or immediate.

Accountability means putting your word and reputation on the line. If failure is not an option, it can feel like too much of responsibility— or a liability—to take on. And there are other cultural factors that thwart accountability in the workplace.

For example, Abraham Zaleznik's classic 1997 HBR article "Real Work" details how conflict and controversy about getting work done is often replaced with politeness, political correctness, ambiguity and attempts to be inoffensive.

This is further supported by John Coleman in his HBR post "Take Ownership of Your Actions by Taking Responsibility," where he describes "Gen Y" as the "coddled" generation. These cohorts were watched over by highly protective "helicopter" parents. As a result, they can tend to see problems as something for others to solve. If people are waiting for others to take action, help may not come. But for those who know how to take action, it's an opportunity.

Some organisations inadvertently encourage slackers. Research indicates that within a group where free riding is the accepted norm, free riders and cheats often get ahead of hard-working members. However, groups of cooperative contributors outperform groups of cheating free riders. This emphasises the reason to hire to your culture first.

## The First Step Towards a Culture of Accountability: Hire for Culture

Since the dominant culture tends to win, it is important to hire for the desired cultural fit. This might seem obvious to some leaders such that they take the suggestion for granted. However, notwithstanding the best of intentions, it's surprising how often organisations unconsciously hire for skills at the expense of hiring for high accountability and cultural fit.

If a leader wants to create a culture of accountability they need recruitment systems that are geared first to high accountability. In high accountability organisations, recruitment specialists have the predicative behavioural tools to not only match technical skills but also assess candidates for both accountability and cultural fit.

## LET'S BRING BACK ACCOUNTABILITY

Author Mills-Scofield illustrates her own experiences with corporate culture and failure:

*"The Bell Labs culture I grew up in had a strong sense of accountability. When you're working on things that literally change the world, it's easy to be committed to something bigger than yourself. The "Labs" culture meant failure was a viable option. Success was discovery and application, not climbing a corporate ladder.*

*"At AT&T, the culture was the opposite. While I was privileged to have great management, the majority of AT&T focused on the bottom line. Failure was not an option."*

*"That's why I believe culture creates ... reasons for people's struggle with accountability."*

**The fear of failure:** As very young children, we're taught failure is bad. What if we can't do it or do it right or something goes wrong? So, as adults, we whittle down the scope, involve others so blame can be shared, make resource requests we know won't fly, and let fear hold us back from really creative solutions.

Since "failure is not an option" is still the modus operandi in most organisations, we find that accepting accountability is still very risky.

But perhaps whilst your organisation has followed best practices in recruitment and selection, it has been burned by extreme examples of failures in organisational accountability such as bullying and harassment. Research indicates that a powerful deterrent to these behaviours can be an explicit agreement made at the time of onboarding between the new hire and the employee that clearly indicates those behaviours which are acceptable and those that won't be tolerated.

Can you change the culture? Yes, over time. But it's best to save yourself the trouble and hire at the outset for high accountability.

*Good interview question*

## The Second Step Towards a Culture of Accountability: Model High Accountability Conversations

So, how do we help our cultures, ourselves, and our people overcome the fear of failure and to commit in an uncertain world? I have a few suggestions based on my experiences in both accountable and unaccountable company cultures.

**Audit your patterns of conversation.** Culture most easily reveals itself in the patterns of conversation that habitually occur across your organisation. Take a close look at the patterns. Better yet, have an independent person sit as an observer in key leadership conversations and document the typical patterns of conversation. Is the dominant pattern high accountability? Where do you fall short? The observer's diagnosis might surprise you. Awareness is the first step in dealing with the issue.

**What do low accountability conversations sound like?** Listen for complaints. There will always be complaining at work; it's how we release negative energy. However, complaints will also reveal what's truly valued. People don't grumble about what they don't care about.

The key to having productive complaints at work is how it evolves. If it ends in negative agreement, as in, "Isn't it awful!" then it shows low accountability. It's non-productive to agree that something is wrong and then not do anything about it.

Low accountability conversations are full of blame and excuses. They end without an assessment of what part the person may have played in the problem. There is usually finger-pointing at forces outside of their control. You can usually see self-serving bias: "I did what I could, but they didn't." The conversation partner listens without asking challenging questions.

You can diagnose low accountability with other conversational symptoms such as silence, avoidance, deferred decision-making, pleasantries, failure to commit, gossip, confusion with direction and expectations, failure to give honest feedback, too much talking and not enough listening, failure to delegate, and failure to give direction and assign responsibility.

**What do high accountability conversations sound like?** High accountability conversations, even when complaints, usually include discussion of causality, but also evaluation of what a person wants to see happen. The person examines how they participate in the problem and what they could do differently. The conversation partner listens and asks questions to help coach the person toward a plan. Earlier in the chapter I outlined many reasons why people may feel it is not safe to engage in high accountability conversation , so it is in a leader's interests to create an environment where it is safe to step up to high accountability.

**Communicate clearly.** How can you expect people to step up if you're not clearly emphasising the company's strategy, mission, and values on a regular basis? People need to tap into something bigger than themselves, and they look to their leaders to reinforce those ideals. Inspire them with a reason to care.

That's only the starting point. Leaders need to translate the big picture into the little steps required to get there. What may seem trivial to people really matters when it's linked to purpose and passion. It's up to leaders to give everyone the vocabulary to repeat the directions themselves. That is how we start changing behaviours and making new habits.

Give your directions some key phrases that can go viral and become a cultural mantra. Teach staff and managers the "language of accountability." Sometimes company-wide shifts happen when leaders give change a name by identifying one habit that ends up trickling down through other behaviours.

Unless people can comfortably speak the language of accountability, they won't easily translate it into long-term cultural change. Training needs to include what to say when colleagues give each other feedback and hold each other accountable.

Feedback needs to fuel progress. There can't be accountability without feedback on what works and what doesn't. Often progress is made through trial and error, but when people are afraid to try because of the consequences of negative feedback and appraisal, nothing gets done and progress stalls.

One of the most difficult communication skills for anyone to master is giving feedback that works. Because of the brain's bias to focus on negative facts, it's challenging to deliver suggestions that are intended to help without seeming to be critical.

## HIGH ACCOUNTABILITY QUESTIONS

To change a conversation from low to high accountability, some key questions to ask are:

- "What part do I play in this situation?"
- "Am I willing to let go of fault, blame and excessive control?"
- "What would I like to see happen?"
- "What would be a reasonable outcome for both me, the other person, and our organisation?"
- "What else can I do?"
- "What needs to happen now?"
- "What am I willing to commit to doing next?"
- "Who will do what, and when?"

Furthermore, this same tendency is at work when we listen to feedback. When we hear several points, we usually remember the negative one most.

Watch how you react to and treat a person, how you discuss feedback with others and how you let it impact that person's future success in the organisation. Your own personal demeanor and handling has an enormous impact.

Make sure that you're present to support a request and to remove or mitigate obstacles. Meet regularly and follow through to identify potential challenges and opportunities before they become a major problem. If it's to become embedded in the culture, accountability requires continual reinforcement and follow-through. It's not a declaration and it's not "one and done."

## GIVE PEOPLE A *CHANGE MANTRA*

Here's how a "change mantra" helped the mid-Atlantic area of Johnson Controls, as reported by authors Craig Hickman, Tom Smith and Roger Connors in their book, *The Oz Principle*.

The company kept losing out to competitors. According to area manager Allen Martin, "People in different departments were so concerned about covering their tails and documenting the things they'd done to prove their value that it really impeded the organisation's ability to be innovative and strategic, and no one was working together to build the business." Market share declined, growth stagnated, morale plunged, and customers grew more and more dissatisfied with the company's performance.

The company decided to work together to build greater accountability around three strategic thrusts:

- Grow 15 percent
- Become number one in the market
- Change the business's value proposition

With their new focus on accountability, everything started to improve. "15, 1, and change" become the cultural mantra of every department. The conversations changed from excuses and finger pointing to, "What else can we do to get the results we want?"

In the three years following, sales more than doubled, profitability tripled, customer satisfaction soared and employee turnover dropped to its lowest level in years. Now, the business is chanting, "25, 1, and change!"

Re-prioritise responsibilities and tasks to allow the person or team to complete the request. Don't just add on. Not everything is urgent and important. As a leader, show your commitment to the request you've made. If it's not worth re-prioritising, then it isn't worth asking.

**Eradicate the failure culture.** Create ways to minimise the stigma of failure. Instead of pointing out *who did what*, focus on what's been learned and how that applies, and what else can be done. Eliminate blame and replace it with responsibility and opportunity.

Recognise the difference between fault and responsibility. We may need to deal with situations that are not our fault (backwards view), but are our responsibility (forward view). Blame inhibits corrective action and undermines learning.

**The problem with feedback.** Marshall Goldsmith, executive coach and best-selling author of *What Got You Here Won't Get You There*, points out that traditional feedback is fundamentally flawed, being typically limited to one dimension—backwards. In experiential exercises with thousands of leaders, he has found that the process of embracing suggestions for future improvement or "feedforward" is equally if not more important in fuelling progress.

## THE DIFFERENCE BETWEEN FAULT AND RESPONSIBILITY

Honda CEO Takanobu Ito demonstrated that concept with his actions after the release of the new Honda Civic when sales expectations quickly fell short, dropping 15 percent. Ito took decisive action, publicly assuming full responsibility for the model's reception. The origination of the failed concept — his or not — did not matter.

All that mattered was claiming ownership of the issue and charting a path forward. Honda quickly followed up by announcing a new release for 2013, a year ahead of the original plan. In the words of executive vice president John Mendel, "... the comments of *Consumer Reports* and our customers have not gone unnoticed. We are appropriately energised."

## Culture Starts at the Top

When employees see a leader standing up to take full responsibility for results, and especially when he or she may not individually be to blame, they see accountability in action. Remember, everything a leader does is noted and often discussed by employees.

When a leader models responsibility, it gives courage to others to step up to the plate. This is one of the key ways accountability takes hold in an organisation's culture. Without leaders who model the behaviour they desire in others, no amount of incentive programs or motivational pep talks will inspire anything but contempt.

Let's look at Southwest Airlines, and how their focus on employee relationships has helped create stellar results in a field where poor results and failures abound.

## SOUTHWEST AIRLINES: RELATIONSHIPS FIRST

Despite following some of the same strategies, no other airline has yet been able to successfully clone Southwest's success:

- In a highly volatile industry, Southwest had been profitable every year except for the year in which it was established. That means by 2003, Southwest had been profitable for 31 years.

- For most of 2002, Southwest's $9 billion market capitalisation exceeded the combined market capitalisation of every other U.S. airline.

- Southwest rated consistently high in *Fortune* Magazine's "100 Best Companies to Work For in America" and from 1992 to 1996 also won the airline industry's "Triple Crown"—the fewest delays, complaints and mishandled bags.

Clearly, Southwest is doing something right. Most attempts to copy Southwest have focused solely on operational issues:

- Flying just one aircraft type—to cut down on training and maintenance costs.

- Using smaller, less congested airports—to avoid schedule disruptions caused by multiple aircraft demands.

- Eliminating meal service and seating assignments—to allow aircraft to be turned around more rapidly.

What's missing is the "secret sauce" Southwest uses to make all these operational factors come together effectively and efficiently.

**SOUTHWEST AIRLINES: RELATIONSHIPS FIRST** *(continued)*

Lying at the heart of the Southwest success story are three elements:

1. 10 organisational practices which **build relationships** between managers and frontline employees and among employees.
2. **An environment** which emphasises shared goals, shared knowledge and mutual respect.
3. **Sound communication techniques** which are frequent, timely and focused on solving problems.

Here is how Southwest summarises their approach to accountability:

| Environment | | 10 Organisational Relationships | Techniques |
|---|---|---|---|
| | 1 | Outstanding business leadership | |
| Shared Goals | 2 | Invest in the front-line leaders | Frequent Communication |
| | 3 | Hire and train for relationship excellence | |
| | 4 | Use conflicts to build relationships | |
| Shared Knowledge | 5 | Bridge the work-family divide | Timely Communication |
| | 6 | Create positions that span boundaries | |
| | 7 | Use broad performance metrics | |
| Mutual Respect | 8 | Highly flexible job descriptions | Problem-Solving Communication |
| | 9 | Partner with the unions | |
| | 10 | Build the supplier relationships | |

The good news is any company that follows the lead of Southwest and builds strong organisational relationships can achieve great success. The bad news is this isn't easy—to achieve it will require making changes on multiple fronts simultaneously. But as in the case of Southwest Airlines, the results can be impressive and long lasting.

> *"For Southwest's leaders, taking care of business literally means taking care of relationships. They see these relationships—with their employees, among their employees, and with outside parties—as the foundation of competitive advantage, through good times and bad. They see the quality of these relationships not as a success factor, but as the most essential success factor. They believe that to develop the company, they must continually invest in these relationships."*
>
> Jody Gittell, author, *The Southwest Airlines Way*

## The Third Step Towards a Culture of Accountability: Establish Keystone Habits

Leaders can change the culture by changing behaviours first. Attitudes will follow. Often, a strategic focus on one behaviour results in companywide improvements. Here's an example involving the habit of handwashing in hospitals.

## EMBED ACCOUNTABILITY AS A CULTURAL NORM: SPECTRUM HEALTH

Every year, 1.7 million Americans are infected and 100,000 die as a result of hospital acquired infections. Researchers and industry regulators have long established that one of the most effective safeguards against HAIs (Healthcare Associated Infection) is proper hand hygiene.

In an effort to decrease hospital infections Spectrum Health, a not-for-profit healthcare system located in Grand Rapids, Michigan, instituted a campaign to boost hand washing among staff from a stalled 60 percent compliance rate.

The campaign included three basic steps:

- **"WIWO:"** Wash in and wash out every time staff enters and exits a patient's room.

- **Hold one another accountable.** Each staff member is 100 percent accountable for both his or her own hand hygiene behaviour and the behaviour of his or her co-workers.

- **Say "Thank You."** When reminded to wash their hands, staff members are to say "thank you for reminding me" and wash again without getting defensive. Staff members should intend to make it safe and easy to remind others.

Within the first two months, Spectrum Health tracked at 90 percent hand hygiene compliance—a 30 percent increase over their benchmark. In 2009, Spectrum Health System reported an unprecedented 98 percent compliance rate.

**EMBED ACCOUNTABILITY AS A CULTURAL NORM:
SPECTRUM HEALTH** *(continued)*

"As people learned to hold each other accountable for something as simple as hand hygiene, they learned the skills to hold each other accountable for other expected outcomes like patient safety, quality, and efficiency," Matt Van Vranken, President of Spectrum Hospital Health Group said. "This initiative has really provided us with a cultural framework to drive high performance broadly across the organisation."

The Clean Hands Program at Spectrum was facilitated by the Vital Smarts team, and it demonstrated sustained success in cleaner hands and lower infection rates.

But the unanticipated consequence was that by developing deep skills in accounting for one's personal hand hygiene, such behaviour was translated into accountability for producing positive results in other areas. Evidence of behaviour change goes beyond hand washing and is visible in the way staff members confront and have the right conversations with one another.

Greater levels of accountability are a fundamental skill, which once embedded into the way we work and relate can be translated into many areas of business. For Spectrum Health, training emphasised that it was perfectly acceptable to remind each other to wash hands, and the only response was "thank you." People were responsible for not only their own behaviour but also for each other's.

This is also an example of the importance of picking one thing to work on. Some habits have the power to start a chain reaction as they move through an organisation. *Keystone habits* are those that identify key priorities that can be leveraged throughout all areas of work. They are habits that the majority of the organisation's people can easily identify with.

You don't have to get every single thing right, just a few significant ones. When you get people to change the key habits that matter the most, they start to shift and dislodge other patterns. Here's an example of how establishing safety as a core strategy brought about five times more productivity and profits.

## CHANGE JUST ONE THING AND GET BIG RESULTS

How does a focus on changing one habit bring big business results? In the book *The Power of Habit*, author Charles Duhigg, writes about the turnaround of the global aluminium corporation, Alcoa. This is an example of how "keystone habits" produce a trickle- down effect across the organisation, translating into profits and productivity.

In 1987, Alcoa faced challenges. One of the largest companies on earth and a pioneer in aluminium smelting, management unwisely tried to expand into new products lines. Competitors were stealing customers and profits away. So most investors were relieved when new leadership was announced.

But they were sceptical when Paul H. O'Neill, former Secretary of Treasury, took the helm. Besides being a government bureaucrat, Wall Street was taken aback when he announced his first strategic plan:

"I want to talk to you about worker safety," he announced. "Every year, numerous Alcoa workers are injured so badly they

## CHANGE JUST ONE THING AND GET BIG RESULTS *(continued)*

miss a day of work. Our safety record is better than the general American workforce, especially considering that our employees work with metals at 1500 degrees and machines that can rip a man's arm off. But it's not good enough. I intend to make Alcoa the safest company in America. I intend to go for zero injuries."

O'Neill hadn't said anything about profits or taxes or government regulations. "If you want to understand how Alcoa is doing, you need to look at our workplace safety figures. If we bring our injury rates down... it will be because the individuals at this company have agreed to become part of something important: They've devoted themselves to creating a habit of excellence. Safety will be an indicator that we're making progress in changing our habits across the entire institution. That's how we should be judged."

Within a year of O'Neill's speech, Alcoa's profits hit a record high. By the time O'Neill retired in 2000, the company's annual net income was five times larger than before he arrived and its market capitalisation had risen by $27 billion.

That growth occurred while Alcoa became one of the safest companies in the world. O'Neill made one of the stodgiest and most potentially dangerous companies into a profit machine by attacking one habit that was key. Other changes followed in a trickle down fashion.

In an interview, O'Neill reported, "I knew I had to transform Alcoa. But you can't order people to change. That's not how the brain works. So I decided I was going to start by focusing on one thing. If I could start disrupting the habits around one thing, it would spread throughout the entire company."

## The Fourth Step Towards a Culture of Accountability: Establish Reinforcing Systems of Accountability

Training is a typical response (and often the only response) to improving accountability in organisations. However, training is not a solution to sustained cultural change. There is little value in training unless it is followed up by reinforcing systems that enable practice in the tools of accountability, i.e., accountable conversations supported by accountability in organisational design, systems, and policy.

The following are a range of interventions that can have a high impact on the reinforcement of a high accountability culture. Certainly they don't all need to be tackled at once unless you intend on embarking on a major program of organisational transformation. In the first instance choose high impact, high value areas in your organisation such as the ones likely to reinforce a keystone habit referred to earlier. High readiness for change and comfort with uncertainty is even better, but not always available.

- Leaders personally educate their staff about accountability conversations and the language of business.

- Critically review elements of organisational design. Reinforce those that enhance high accountability and minimise those that perpetuate low accountability.

  - Eliminate unnecessary organisational silos and create roles that span traditional boundaries.
  - Encourage cross-functional team collaboration and client collaboration.

- Reduce bureaucratic hierarchies to enable more authority in decision making and easier flow of communication between and across organisational levels and boundaries.
- Invest greater authority in front line staff who make decisions closer to the point of value (i.e., directly with the consumer).
- Empower staff by training everyone in the language of business, thereby encouraging participation in meaningful discussions about business performance and strategy.
- Focus more on broad metrics of performance and potential rather than punitive measures of retrospective progress and failure.
- Balance constructive feedback on past performance with feedforward on future possibilities and follow-through on task assignments.
- Create broad job descriptions that enable innovation and flow.
- Apply motivational principles to reward and recognition that encourage high accountability, thereby minimising outmoded carrot and stick incentives.
- Ensure hiring practices prioritise the recruitment of new staff for high accountability.
- Audit organisational policies for unnecessary bureaucracy and control.
- Engage in meaningful partnering and high accountability conversations with unions rather than adversarial posturing.
- Engage in participative goal setting.
- Assign a RACI matrix to each role that clearly establish responsibility and accountability for each position.

## RESPONSIBILITY MATRICES (RACI)

**A responsibility assignment matrix (RAM),** also known as **RACI matrix or linear responsibility chart (LRC),** describes the participation by various roles in completing tasks or deliverables for a project or business process. It is especially useful in clarifying roles and responsibilities in cross-functional/departmental projects and processes.

RACI is an acronym that was derived from the four key responsibilities most typically used: *Responsible, Accountable, Consulted, and Informed.*

*Source: Wikipedia.org.*

# Pulling It Together

In Chapter 1, I suggested that leaders are ultimately responsible for creating accountability throughout the organisation. How they handle mistakes, blame, accountability, and credit is observed and modeled by the employees.

What leaders say and do matters. Leaders can't get others to give their best if they aren't sincere and congruent with their own actions and words. They set up accountability systems and processes—but none of them will work unless trust is solid.

In Chapter 2, we reviewed some of the main theories about how managers motivate people for greater engagement in their jobs. We also discussed why many incentive and pay-for-performance programs don't work or produce poor results. You'll need to be aware of these concepts as you decide what kind of accountability plan will work for your people in your organisation.

In Chapter 3, I discussed how consequences work. How can you set up processes so that a consequence is motivating for the right results? How can you discourage poor performance? What obstacles and barriers are common? And in this chapter, Chapter 4, we saw that no matter how much you encourage individuals to take responsibility, the organisation needs to enable the right culture for any of it to work. A culture of accountability is actionable and requires work. Here we presented four steps to creating an accountability culture, and we reviewed several case studies where organisations have changed their culture to surmount problems and thrive.

Now, in Chapter 5, it's time to wrap it all up.

# Checklist for
# High Accountability Culture

☑ Audit your culture by auditing your conversations.

☑ Establish training modeled by leaders in accountability conversations and the language of business.

☑ Hire to a high accountability culture.

☑ Identify keystone habits.

☑ Review key organisational structures, systems and policies, reinforce high accountability and minimise drivers of low accountability.

☑ Create your accountability plan.

# CHAPTER 5

# Wrapping It All Up–Feedback, Feedforward, and Follow Through

**H**ow do you instill a culture of accountability throughout the organisation and get people working in harmony to achieve desired business results?

The answer to this key question is somewhat of a mystery. Like great art, you'll know it when you see it. As a leader, as a manager, and as a contributing member to the organisation, it's a question you need to continually be asking of yourself.

Despite the ever-shifting nature of the question, there can be answers and steps to be taken. Some you won't like because they involve giving up control. Some you will like (a lot!) because they truly work for getting people engaged with their work.

Multiple surveys by Gallup and other organisations show that the greatest untapped potential in every company are the two-thirds of non-engaged people who show up each day and go through the motions without really contributing their intelligence and skills.

You can't tell anyone to use their imaginations and energy; they have to want to give it. You can't command someone to show initiative or be creative. Those are literally gifts that people choose to bring into work every day—or not.

Gary Hamel says it best:

> "The question a manager needs to ask himself is not 'How do I get people to serve my company?' but rather, *How do I create the work environment and a sense of purpose that literally merits the gifts of creativity and passion?*"

In this book, I suggest you look at accountability from three perspectives:

- **Leadership accountability.** How do leaders model accountability and inspire their people? How are they responsible for attitudes and mindset, blame and fault vs. responsibility? How should they be communicating to their followers?

- **Personal accountability.** What ways can individuals participate in accountability programs? What drives and motivates individuals? How do incentives and consequences work?

- **Cultural accountability.** How does accountability spread or get squashed throughout the organisation? How do you get peers to hold each other accountable? What is the language of accountability? How can keystone habits create culture-wide shifts and business results?

I explore the current research on motivation, incentives, and outline a three-pronged approach that promotes better accountability throughout the organisation based on:

A. Clear communications.
B. Compelling consequences.
C. Conversations that promote cultural accountability.

It wasn't until I was finishing the final drafts of this book that a good catch-phrase came to me summarising these ideas for *Accountability Leadership*: feedback, feedforward and follow through.

## Feedback, Feedforward, and Follow Through

While this is simplified for greater retention, it's far from simple to implement, as you can imagine. Accountability is a wide-reaching component of sustainable competitive advantage. Without it, productivity slips, or the wrong things are achieved without the right results.

Accountability is not a vague and fuzzy feel-good management fad. It is every leader's responsibility to take a long hard look at accountability in their organisation and do everything possible to instill a program that works.

Accountability is actionable, possible, improvable, and crucial. Don't let these or any good ideas fall by the wayside. Take action, get informed, and find out what's going on in your company and where the accountability gaps are.

Why? Because there are gaps in your organisation. You can be sure of that. They just may not be where you think they are. While I'm a consultant and my job is to help leaders achieve the results they want and are capable of, I'm not preaching accountability to get more clients.

I've written this book because time after time smart leaders admit to me they are often baffled by accountability. They tell me that they know how much they need the participation and passion of all of their people, but they're not sure the best ways to unleash their full potential.

They know many people languish in their jobs because they don't feel the same purpose and passion the leaders do. Leaders really do want to give their people meaning and fulfillment at work—they just aren't sure how to inspire them and to reach their hearts as well as their minds.

I'm going to repeat myself a little bit. Here's what I said in my introduction, and it is still true:

## GOOD IDEAS ARE NOT ENOUGH

My wish is that by reading this book, you'll identify areas where you can improve your accountability leadership. More than that, I hope you'll not rest satisfied by the discovery of "good ideas."

Why? I say this because "good ideas" don't last. When they turn into damn hard work, they get abandoned by the very people who need them the most.

Don't let this happen to you. Take action; put these good ideas into your daily leadership strategies and into a tangible, measurable Accountability Plan for personal and organisational improvement. After all, what gets measured gets done!

Like many leadership development specialists who work with smart executives, I encourage you to be among the small percentage who muster the courage to take on this challenging work of accountability improvement.

You'll be glad you did, because you'll see the results clearly. It's not some vague feel-good approach to an empathy-based management fad of the month.

This is real. This works. It always has, only the key required elements have slightly changed with the evolving nature of 21st century business, economics, and knowledge workers.

If you think things are tough now, you may not be prepared for the accelerating pace ahead. Read this now, then do what you need to do. Call your coach. Make a plan, start improving your accountability leadership and the accountability culture of your organisation.

In summary, take steps to give g*ood feedback, feedforward,* and *follow through.*

Take courage in the knowledge your systems will work better with clarity and repetition.

But above all, take action to improve the accountability of yourself and your teams.

Here's to your accountability journey!

*Di Worrall*

**di@diworrall.com.au**

P.S. In the pipeline is the *Accountability Leadership Field Guide.* It will give you exercises, checklists, and questions to work through. Based on the concepts I've presented here, you will gain clarity about the current state of accountability and responsibility in your organisation, revealing previously untapped opportunities for personal and business transformation using the *new* science of accountability.

# References

## Introduction

Quote: Mihnea Moldoveanu from *"The Promise: The Basic Building Block of Accountability"* (Rotman Magazine, Fall 2009).

Poor performance & lack of trust: CIA; Aldrich Ames case material: Kennedy School of Government Case Program C115-96-1339.1—*James Woolsey and the CIA: The Aldrich Ames Spy Case (Sequel)*.

Missed deadlines and cost overruns:

1. *Flawed, failed, abandoned: 100 P3s, Canadian & International Evidence.* Natalie Mehra Ontario Health Coalition 2005; http://archive.cupe.ca/updir/Flawed_Failed_Abandoned_-_Final.pdf

2. *Executive Politics, Risk and the Mega-Project Paradox,* Will Jennings. http://www.academia.edu/532779/Executive_Politics_Risk_and_the_Mega-Project_Paradox

Questionable Ethics: Graves, Sharron M., and Stephen F. Austin. *"Student Cheating Habits: A Predictor Of Workplace Deviance."* Journal of Diversity Management 3.1 (2008): 15-22.

Stopping Corporate Misdeeds: How we teach the wrong lessons. Excerpted from *What were they thinking? Unconventional Wisdom about management* by Jeffrey Pfeiffer Harvard Business School Press, Boston Massachusetts (2007).

Chronic inefficiency: http://www.medicinestransparency.org/key-issues/transparency-and-accountability/.

Poor customer satisfaction: *"Leadership Under Pressure: Communication is Key."* Jose R Pin, IEE Insight, Fourth Quarter 2012.

Poor safety: *Flawed, failed, abandoned: 100 P3s, Canadian & International Evidence.* Natalie Mehra Ontario Health Coalition 2005: http://archive.cupe.ca/updir/Flawed_Failed_Abandoned_-_Final.pdf.

## Chapter 1: Accountability for Leaders

Accountability vs. Responsibility: *A Climate for Change,* by Di Worrall (2009).

The Majority of Workers Are Disengaged: Gallup research: http://www.gallup.com/services/176300/state-global-workplace.aspx.

Employees First, Customers Second: Vineet Nayar authored a book about his groundbreaking accountability program as CEO of HCL Technologies. http://amzn.com/1422139069.

Top Down Accountability: HCL Technologies Pave the Way: An excellent article about HCL Technologies in Harvard Business Review, June, 2010: https://hbr.org/2010/06/how-i-did-it-a-maverick-ceo-explains-how-he-persuaded-his-team-to-leap-into-the-future.

Clarity: Simon Sinek writes and speaks about this in his TED Talk, "Start with Why." See also his book, *Start with Why: How Great Leaders Inspire Everyone to Take Action* (Portfolio, 2010).

Millions Quit Their Jobs: see links in the call out box for survey data.

Praise + Recognition: Gallup Research: http://www.gallup.com/services/176301/state-global-workplace.aspx.

65 potential incentives in the workplace: Dr. Gerald Graham of Wichita State University.

Building Trust: James Robbins in *Nine Minutes on Monday,* McGraw Hill Education, 2012.

Negativity Bias: For a good summary, see Wikipedia: https://en.wikipedia. org/wiki/Negativity_bias.

Feedforward: This article about how to use feedforward is from the Marshall Goldsmith Library: http://www.marshallgoldsmithfeedforward.com/html/Articles.htm.

## Chapter 2: The Science of Motivation
Simon Sinek, *Start with Why: How Great Leaders Inspire Others to Act,* (Portfolio, 2009).

In-the-box, out-of-the-box thinking: *Leadership and Self-Deception by The Arbinger Institute,* Berrett-Koehler; Second Edition edition (January 11, 2010).

Above the line, below the line experiences: *The Oz Principle,* by Roger Connors, Tom Smith, and Craig Hickman (Portfolio, 2004).

*Level 5 Leadership* (2009) and *Good to Great: Why Some Companies Make the Leap... And Others Don't* (2001) by Jim Collins, HarperBusiness.

Rewards do not create a lasting commitment. Rewards typically undermine the very processes they are intended to enhance: Deci, E.L., *Intrinsic Motivation*, Plenum Publishing 1975.

An attitude of accountability: *The Oz Principle*, by Roger Connors, Tom Smith, and Craig Hickman (Portfolio, 2004).

Hawthorne studies of the early 30s:
http://en.wikipedia.org/wiki/Hawthorne_studies.

*How do you motivate people?* Frederick Herzberg:
https://numerons.files.wordpress.com/2012/04/how-do-you-motivate-employees-frederick-herzberg.pdf.

Creating Flow Conditions: Mihaly Csikszentmihalyi
https://en.wikipedia. org/wiki/Mihaly_Csikszentmihalyi.

"flow": https://en.wikipedia.org/wiki/Flow_(psychology).

Autonomy: read more about how people desire control over their work in Daniel H. Pink *Drive, The Surprising Truth About What Motivates Us* (Riverhead) 2011.

"Your greatest source of power for creating compelling consequences:" Jeff Grimshaw and Gregg Baron in *Leadership without Excuses: How to Create Accountability and High Performance (Instead of Just Talking About It)*, McGraw-Hill, 2010.

## *Chapter 3: Compelling Consequences*
"People don't conform to the logic of traditional economics:" Nobel Prize laureates Daniel Kahneman and Amos Tversky.

List your consequence capital: Jeff Grimshaw and Gregg Baron in *Leadership without Excuses: How to Create Accountability and High Performance (Instead of Just Talking About It)*, McGraw-Hill, 2010.

Loss aversion: In economics and decision theory, loss aversion refers to people's tendency to strongly prefer avoiding losses to acquiring gains. Some studies suggest that losses are twice as powerful, psychologically, as gains. Loss aversion was first convincingly demonstrated by Amos Tversky and Daniel Kahneman. See http://en.wikipedia.org/wiki/Loss_aversion.

The Progress Principle: Research and book authored by Teresa Amabile and Steven Kramer, *The Progress Principle: Using Small Wins to Ignite Joy, Engagement, and Creativity at Work* (Harvard Business Press, 2011).

Leadership Trust Deficit: From the 2011 Maritz Survey, Press archive, *"Americans Still Lack Trust In Company Management Post Recession."*

Leadership Trust Survey: Article by Robert Hurley in https://hbr.org/2006/09/the-decision-to-trust

Watson Wyatt Worldwide: http://www.towerswatson.com.

## Chapter 4: Creating a Culture of Accountability

Quote, "Where does accountability start?" Mihnea Moldoveanu, *"The Promise. The Basic Building Block of Accountability"* (Rotman Magazine Fall 2009).

"But if that's not accompanied by a systematic effort to create conditions of accountability...": Jeff Grimshaw and Gregg Baron in *Leadership without Excuses: How to Create Accountability and High Performance* (McGraw Hill, 2010).

For a refresher course on measurements of accountability, read Nassim Taleb's *Fooled by Randomness (Random House, 2005)* and Phil Rosenzweig's *Halo Effect (Free Press, 2014).*

The Halo Effect: see http://en.wikipedia.org/wiki/Halo_effect.

Edward Thorndike, an American psychologist: for a review of his accomplishments, see http://en.wikipedia.org/wiki/Edward_Thorndike.

Correlation and causation: For a review of common errors in reading statistics, see http://en.wikipedia.org/wiki/Correlation_and_causation.

Obstacles in creating a culture of accountability: Harvard Business Review blog post, *"Let's Bring Back Accountability,"* July 30, 2012, Deborah Mills-Scofield.

Dealing with conflict and being too polite: Abraham Zaleznik's classic 1997 HBR article *"Real Work"* http://hbr.org/1997/11/real-work/ar/1.

Accountability and the younger generations: see John Coleman in his HBR post *"Take Ownership of Your Actions by Taking Responsibility,"* https://hbr.org/2012/08/take-ownership-of-your-actions.

Give People a Change Mantra: *The Oz Principle*, by Roger Connors, Tom Smith, and Craig Hickman (Portfolio, 2004).

The difference between fault and responsibility: Honda Civic example: https://hbr.org/2012/08/take-ownership-of-your-actions.

Southwest Airlines example: *The Southwest Airlines Way: Using the Power of Relationships to Achieve High Performance*, author Dr. Jody Gittell, McGraw Hill Education, 2005.

Embed accountability as a cultural norm: Spectrum Health example by Vitalsmarts: http://www.vitalsmarts.com/casestudies/spectrum-health/.

Keystone habits, change one big thing: *The Power of Habit*, author Charles Duhigg, Random House, 2012.

Story of Alcoa attributed to Charles Duhigg in *The Power of Habit*. See also http://en.wikipedia.org/wiki/Alcoa.

Responsibility Matrices (RACI): http://en.wikipedia.org/wiki/Responsibility_assignment_matrix.

## Chapter 5: Wrapping It All Up

Gary Hamel quote from *What Matters Now: How to Win in a World of Relentless Change, Ferocious Competition, and Unstoppable Innovation*. See author's page, Gary Hamel on Amazon.

# ABOUT THE AUTHOR

**D**i Worrall is an award-winning business transformation executive, change management consultant, and executive coach to the world's most senior business leaders. She is also a published author and leading voice in the global movement of organisational change.

Over the course of her career, she's developed a personal and professional mantra about what she sees as the number-one issue that makes or breaks leadership performance today: **Accountability** for outcomes, performance, and results.

That mantra goes like this:

*"The degree to which you have developed the capacity to hold your organisation and its people accountable for the delivery of results is **directly proportional** to your capacity to either build—or hemorrhage—value from your organisation."*

## An Early Accountability Lesson Becomes a Catalyst for Change

In her first senior executive post, Di managed to turn a difficult accountability lesson into an opportunity for change when it became clear that the failure of her executive team to hold one another accountable was setting their entire organisation up to fail on its delivery of a major business initiative.

Having no intention of letting the project go bad, Di led her fellow executives through specific actions to improve personal accountability throughout the leadership team. As a result, she and the senior team managed to turn a pending loss into a remarkable profit.

"Accountability was something we couldn't delegate," she says, recalling the initiative. "Much to our surprise, employees in our respective divisions started to intuitively follow suit, modelling our new behaviours."

Inspired by that early experience, Di developed a deep curiosity and drive to understand the "new science" of high accountability. This led her to create the best seller *Accountability Leadership*—the first in a range of titles from The Accountability Code® series of books, workshops, information products and trainings.

## Extensive Experience and Expertise

With over 20 years' experience leading programs of business strategy, business transformation, organisational change and strategic human resources at the enterprise level, Di's professional background and knowledge spans a range of industries—public and private—both in Australia and abroad.

These include:

- More than 10 years as senior executive and group director of large government and private multinationals;

- Over 10 years working with senior leaders as principal of business transformation consultancy, Worrall and Associates.

## Thought Leadership and Published Works

Di's extensive experience and thought leadership in end-to-end business transformation, change management, executive coaching and workplace accountability has inspired the creation of a range of published works, including:

- **http://www.diworrall.com.au/leadingchangeblog**—a blog for leaders of change and business transformation

- *A Climate for Change: How to Ride the Wave of Change into the 21st Century* (2009) D Worrall

- *Babes in Business Suits: Top Women Entrepreneurs Share Success Secrets* (2009) F Pizzonia, D Worrall

- *Accountability Leadership: How Great Leaders Build a High Performance Culture of Accountability and Responsibility* (2013) Di Worrall. Available in e-book, paperback and audiobook formats.

- *The Personal Accountability Code—The Step-by-Step Guide to a Winning Strategy that Transforms Your Goals into Reality with the New Science of Personal Accountability* (2014) Di Worrall.

## In the Pipeline

*Accountability Leadership* is the first title in The Accountability Code® series. Upcoming titles include:

- *Accountability Leadership: The Field Guide*

- *The Accountability Code Workshop—Facilitator's Guide and Participant Handbook for building a high performance culture of accountability and responsibility in the workplace.*

# EXCLUSIVE BONUS FOR READERS OF ACCOUNTABILITY LEADERSHIP

**C**lick on the link below for your exclusive bonus access to a twenty-minute podcast interview where business journalist Phil Dobbie interviews world renowned thought leader and executive coach Marshall Goldsmith.

Marshall has sold over a million copies of *New York Times* and *Wall Street Journal* best sellers such as *What Got You Here Won't Get You There*, and thousands have attended his famous leadership seminars on feedforward. In 2013, Marshall was nominated as the number one leadership thinker in the world at the prestigious bi-annual Thinkers50 ceremony sponsored by the Harvard Business Review.

We ask Marshall the question:

> *If a leader's number one challenge is to hold others to account for the delivery of results, why do leaders so often get it wrong, and what can be done to bridge the gap?*

http://www.diworrall.com.au/marshallgoldsmithpodcast

# ADDITIONAL RESOURCES
# FROM DI WORRALL

## Questions and Comments

Email me at **di@diworrall.com.au**

## Receive the Leading Change newsletter

Sign up for Di Worrall's free e-zine *Leading Change*—for leaders of business transformation and change at
**www.diworrall.com.au**

## Need Consulting Advice?

Whether you need consulting advice to transform your business operating model; a facilitator for your strategic planning retreat; or an Interim Executive to lead the design and deployment of a program of end-to-end enterprise transformation; our services in business transformation and change consulting can help achieve your strategic objectives. Contact us at **enquiry@diworrall.com.au** or visit **www.diworrall.com.au**

## Secure Your Personal Executive Coach

If your goal is to enhance your personal leadership performance and career progression, or you have the responsibility to improve the performance of other leaders in your organisation, our executive coaching program might be for you. Find out why our globally recognised coaching program consistently achieves a 95% success rate, enabling successful leaders to get even better through sustained behavioural change and proven leadership growth. For a confidential consultation contact **di@diworrall.com.au**

## One Last Thing...

If you have found something of value by reading this book, I would be grateful if you would post a simple note to friends and colleagues. I would also be honoured if you would post a positive review on Amazon.

To your success!

Di Worrall

Made in the USA
Monee, IL
17 February 2022